A Priest Forever

Ordained

three hours

before he died,

he remains...

A Priest Forever

The Life of
Father Eugene Hamilton

FR. BENEDICT J. GROESCHEL, C.F.R.
FOREWORD BY JOHN CARDINAL O'CONNOR

Our Sunday Visitor Publishing Division
Our Sunday Visitor, Inc.
Huntington, Indiana 46750

Contents

Acknowledgments

The first-time writing of a biography can only be the joint effort of many people. All the material on the subject is fresh and new. Writing a first-time biography can be and in this case was an adventure and a deeply moving experience. I am profoundly indebted to Father Eugene Hamilton's own family — his parents, Deacon Eugene and Margaret Burns Hamilton, and his brother, Tom. They moved beyond their own sorrow and loss and willingly accepted the pain of going over so many details. Many close friends and associates of Father Gene — spiritual directors and guides, teachers and fellow students, friends and peers — generously responded to my request for significant remembrances. At times I had to be selective with the material because it repeated a theme in Father Gene's life, like generosity or faith. If I had included all the information I had at hand the book would have been too long and would have become unfocused.

Several people played a significant role in Gene's life and ordination. For the most part I have used their own words, directly citing their accounts because they were written, in all cases, from the heart. Rather than list them here, let me simply thank all who responded to the request for memories of Father Gene. Those who made significant contributions are obvious from the text.

Apart from the text it is only appropriate to acknowledge our Holy Father Pope John Paul II; Pio Cardinal Laghi, Prefect of the Congregation for Catholic Education; John Cardinal O'Connor; Archbishop Edwin O'Brien, now Coadjutor Archbishop of the Military Archdiocese; and the faculty of St. Joseph's Seminary, without whom Gene would not have achieved the priesthood. This book would have been written even without Father Gene's ordination, both as a tribute to him and as an attempt to capture in words the vocation of an extraordinary young man. But the fact that he was ordained casts a powerful light on his own personal journey to God and, I think, on the Catholic priesthood itself.

I am deeply grateful to my faithful and patient literary co-operator James Monti, who not only typed the entire manuscript but also offered invaluable assistance with research. I am also very grateful for the providential assistance of the eminent Father Avery Dulles, S.J., who offered his theological insights on the nature of priesthood.

Finally, I will ever be grateful to Father Eugene Hamilton. This is a book inside a book, and I have amply quoted from his own writings, especially his unfinished manuscript, striving to leave out no significant words. These quotations are filled with light, love, and beauty. No book I have ever written has moved me more personally than this work because of Gene's own writings and words. After many years of life as a priest, I must confess that I will never look at life or the priesthood in quite the same way. Gene has put the Christian and priestly vocation in a new light for me and apparently for many other people who knew him — priests, religious, laity, teachers, fellow students, medical staff, Catholics, and non-Catholics alike. Though I did not know him long or very well, I will always be grateful to God that I knew him at all. I hope by this work you will come to know him better or for the first time, and that you also will be changed.

Father Benedict Joseph Groeschel, C.F.R.

Trinity Retreat, Larchmont, New York

June 21, 1997

Anniversary of the Death of St. Aloysius Gonzaga

Introduction

Even to write his name as *Father* Eugene Hamilton awes me because of its improbability. This is a young man whose formal seminary training was minimal, whose struggle for life meant literally fighting for breath and whose hope for ordination to the priesthood seemed a mere fantasy. Yet he was ordained, never to "function" as a priest, but to *be* a priest forever, "after the Order of Melchisedeck," within moments of his death. How could this be? This is the question Father Benedict is really addressing in this work.

In my own judgement, the answer is twofold, both components ultimately enfolded, of course, in the mystery of Divine Providence itself. The first lies in the life, the vision, the commitment, and the perseverance of both Eugene Hamilton and his family. Father Benedict elucidates the respective roles of son and parents most movingly.

The second and critical component that made the ordination possible was the extraordinary generosity of our Holy Father, Pope John Paul II, and the Pope's personal love of the priesthood. As a philosopher, he believes thoroughly in the *ontological* nature of the priesthood, as *Pastores Dabo Vobis* makes clear. A man is not merely invited to put on a set of vestments or authorized to serve in a particular capacity, with the new title of "Father." He *becomes* a priest. A spiritually ontological change takes place in his very being, so that while he looks and walks and talks as before, now he *is* a priest.

Hence, our Holy Father did not seem concerned that Eugene would never function as a priest, *except in his very being*. It was enough, in other words, that he *be* a priest.

It was His Eminence, Pio Cardinal Laghi, Prefect of the Congregation for Catholic Education (of Seminaries and other Institutes of Studies), whose thoughtful approval of the request presented to him even preceded his seeking the concurrence of our Holy Father. The Church in New York will be long in his debt for this goodness.

I, personally, thank Father Benedict for a story of inspiration in an all-too-cynical world.

John Cardinal O'Connor
Archbishop of New York

Preface

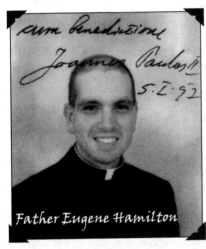

Father Eugene Hamilton

This book fulfills a promise made to an exceptionally fine young man who would be gone from this world in less than six hours. He himself had written part of a book about his own calling to the priesthood and his struggle to answer it in the face of terminal cancer. He hoped to be a priest long enough to preach to others, bearing witness to the graces that he had received, I might add, with great generosity and humility. I vividly recall my last words to him, spoken during a phone call from California, a hurried conversation while he was gasping for breath and had to return to his oxygen mask — "Gene, you will preach your sermon . . . I will see to it."

This book is a labor of love, a fulfillment of a promise made in the most solemn circumstances imaginable — the beginnings of the hour of death. In the following six hours on January 24, 1997, almost incredible things were to happen — much more for the benefit of others than for Gene himself. But these events were to fulfill the hopes of a short, and in many ways exceptional, life.

My first real conversation with Eugene Hamilton stands out in my mind very clearly. I had heard of this student who was so ill with cancer and who was so brave about it all. Hearing of Gene's devotion to Terence Cardinal Cooke (archbishop of New York from 1965 until he died in 1983; made a cardinal in 1969), I had stopped by to pray with him at Good Samaritan Hospital in Suffern, New York. As postulator of the cause for sainthood of Cardinal Cooke, it seemed something of a responsibility for me to pray with this earnest young devotee.

Gene was worn out that day and very much feeling the effects of recent chemotherapy. Our conversation was brief, with most of the time spent praying with Gene and his mother. I recall leaving the hospital deeply impressed by the faith and trust of this tragically sick young seminarian.

Our first real conversation took place later, when I came to teach a class at St. Joseph's Seminary of the New York Archdiocese. He found me in the front corridor and wanted to talk and pray. Gene shared his catastrophic medical condition with me in the most matter-of-fact and understated way, but explained he had chosen to keep his terminal condition a secret from all except a select group. We spoke of Cardinal Cooke, for whom he had such great admiration, and also of his acceptance of God's will — whatever that was to be. Gene mentioned that he was much inspired by Cardinal Cooke's own patience and acceptance of God's will over a period of nine years, also in the face of terminal cancer.

Finally, Gene spoke very gently of his belief that he was going to be a priest, adding that this was very problematic unless he was cured. We prayed to Our Lord and Our Lady, asking the intercession of Cardinal Cooke, at the end of our meeting. It struck me then that these prayers were offered without any human expectation of fulfillment, only complete reliance on God and His mysterious providence. The motto of Cardinal Cooke — "Thy Will Be Done" — was in the minds of both of us.

Eugene probably did not realize how deeply moved I was

by this half-hour spent together. The color of death was upon him. His hair was short and very thin because of chemotherapy. His eyes had lost the sparkle that one sees in his college photographs. Instead, there was a deep and arresting intensity in those dark eyes, an intensity that one sometimes observes in those who are facing the mystery of terminal illness squarely, and unlike most of the rest of humanity, have looked beyond what human sight can see.

After our conversation, I paused at the threshold of the majestic seminary chapel. I recall saying to myself, perhaps half-audibly, "Different . . . this young man is very different." I need to mention here that there are many aspects of life about which I know little or nothing. Current styles, cars, TV, computers, even athletics are blanks to me. But I have studied people for almost four decades, and thus I feel some justification in saying that this dying young man was different. He had a center of gravity, a simplicity of direction, a certitude of purpose, a faith that was not intimidated by the clear approach of death. The vast majority of people — even religious people — could not display a certitude like this, or at least to this degree.

As I walked away from the chapel I came quietly to two conclusions: namely, that God would be with Eugene, and that all would be well. Perhaps there would be a miraculous cure. More than one had been reported, and even announced, by medical doctors in the cause of Cardinal Cooke.

Perhaps. . . . He was sure he was going to be a priest, but he was only taking his first theology class and missing most of his other classes now because of illness. He was so young and so far from completing the required four years of theology that there was no hope of ordination without some kind of intervention of God's providence.

In the midst of these thoughts, the word kept running through my mind — different, different, different. It came to me, then, that the word "different" is the root meaning of the word "holy." *Sanctus* in Latin, *Hagios* in Greek, *Kodesh* in Hebrew — they all mean that God is different — transcendently beyond our thoughts and expectations, mysteriously the plenitude of being: "For as the heavens are higher than the earth, so are my ways higher than your ways and my thoughts than your thoughts" (Isaiah 55:9).

In the coming months many people would come to see that this young man was "different." I don't mean simply an excellent student, an engaging personality, an extraordinarily kind and caring person, a deeply devout Christian, and a dedicated candidate for the priesthood in these shabby and unbelieving times. He was in fact all of these things. But these qualities were not enough to explain my sense of his being different that day outside St. Joseph's Chapel. He was different because the "hand of the Lord was upon him" and he was responding from the very depths of his being.

This little book is about the different, the mysterious, the sacred, about the presence and action of God as He accomplishes His unsearchable will in the ordinary events of life. It is about the sacramental and the sacred, the eternal priesthood of Christ, and how these transcendent realities unfold before human eyes in a world of the familiar, of high school, basketball, proms, exams, and biopsies. When the eternal and the temporal come together, the spirit and the flesh, the human and divine, one finds the sacramental. That's what sacraments are, divine gifts operating in the web of time and matter. This is a story of the sacraments — all seven — but it is especially a glimpse at the priesthood.

If you have limited your view of life to what can be weighed and measured in some way, don't read another word of this book. If you are skeptical about God's presence and operation in the lives of ordinary people, if you are a victim of the purely rationalistic view of life (blind as that is), and can only accept what the limited human mind can comprehend, get rid of this book. It will only bore or annoy you. If baptism is for you just a rite of initiation, the Eucharist a shared sacred meal, and the priesthood only a function, don't read any further, because this is an account of a young man who believed he was called to be a priest forever. If you are skeptical about the sacramental, you will see his ordination as a mistake, and estimate that he was a useless clergyman for less than three hours. But if you are willing to bow your neck before the mystery of God, if you see all of life as a sacramental encounter between Divinity and humanity, between Creator and creature, between Christ and the members of His Mystical Body, then you will be enriched by the message of this book, and you will be deeply moved by the fact that Eugene Hamilton in the hour of death became a priest forever.

1

A Gentle Sign of Contradiction

Gene as an infant

The town of Haverstraw, about twenty-five miles north of the big city in the heart of the Hudson Valley, is everything that people think that New York is not. It's a million miles away culturally and psychologically from that city which the Pope called the capital of the world. In fact, many surrounding towns and even some sections of New York City itself are far removed from the worldly, competitive, and often cynical metropolitan whirl. The average New Yorker (if such a creature can be imagined) is far more traditional and religious, far more a homebody, than most of the rest of the world would assume. Haverstraw has always been a blue-collar town, famous for making millions of bricks that would be shipped out by river barges to build New York City. It is a town of modest homes, of people struggling to earn their daily bread and a little bit extra for their children. Despite the presence of some ugly industrial plants, the beauty of the valley and the river, and the quaint old Victorian buildings make it a pleasant haven for commuters and a fairly safe place for a young family to grow. Eugene's father was born here, and his mother came from a similar town, Port Chester, on the shores of Long Island Sound. Like Cardinal Cooke, whom Gene so admired, the family descended from the Irish immigrants who make up that still fascinating subculture.

Eugene was born in a time of immense social, cultural, and religious change. The quiet river town, Haverstraw, by the time of his birth had developed a vibrant Spanish-speaking Latin-

Gene Sr., Cardinal Cooke, Margaret, Eugene, and Tom at Gene Sr.'s ordination as a permanent deacon in St. Patrick's Cathedral on May 1, 1982.

American population. Almost a symbol of the changes coming to this world was an Irish American priest, Father Edward Keehan, who served the needs of the Spanish-speaking citizens for a number of years before Gene was born. The opening of the Tappan Zee Bridge joining Rockland County with a direct link with the city, along with television, shopping malls, and economic prosperity, brought many changes to the Hudson Valley. In the late '60s and early '70s new ways of thinking shook every institution in society, including the Catholic Church, which was struggling at the same time to assimilate the changes of Vatican II in a general atmosphere of cultural dislocation. In the midst of these changes, Eugene Hamilton, Sr., then working his way up as an auditor for the Internal Revenue Service, and his wife Margaret, a teacher who had been a Sister of Charity for a few years, welcomed into the world their two sons, Eugene and Thomas. Although a traditional and active Catholic couple, the changes in the Church would affect them in ways totally unforeseen. At least one of these ways was very positive. On May 1, 1982, Gene Sr. was ordained a permanent deacon of the Catholic Church by Terence Cardinal Cooke in St. Patrick's Cathedral.

In this challenging world of change, Gene Sr., and Margaret were able to provide a devout and stable home for their two young sons. A touching event was recalled by their seminarian son when he wrote a spiritual autobiography for the seminary. His mother had taken the two-year-old to Mass on the First Sunday of Advent, and as the celebrant lit the first Advent candle the boy began to sing out with full voice "Happy Birthday." His mother was embarrassed, but everyone else was delighted.

Early in Gene's life we find two elements that are symbolic, if not prophetic, of the future. The first was a very positive embracing of the Catholic faith by those around him. The Hamiltons took full advantage of the existence of a spiritual resource located almost in their back yard. The Marian Shrine had been opened by the Salesians in West Haverstraw in the 1950s. By this time, following the inspiration of their founder St. John Bosco, they were providing a wide range of services for children and families. The boys went to nursery school there and stayed on in the summer basketball program. Gene later would describe this powerful influence on his vocation in a thirteen-page spiritual autobiography, written as part of his entrance requirements for the St. John Neumann Residence and dated January 5, 1994:

> At the Shrine, there was an integration of faith and fun. Basketball was followed by Mass, which was followed by lunch. The afternoons brought more basketball and fun. It was the presence of these priests and brothers who worked for youth and their enthusiasm that sustained my positive yet realistic image of the priesthood and religious life. At that time in my life I was becoming aware of the humanity of priests as well. The Salesians were shining examples of individuals happy about serving God and His people. My devotion and reliance on Mary also increased in these years. The Shrine provided me with many opportunities to reflect upon her life and her calling as the Mother of God.[1]

Gene later would recall three Salesians who had a special influence on him: Brother Tom Higgs, S.D.B., who is still at the Shrine; Father Richard McCormick, S.D.B., who is now a high school principal, having served as provincial; and Father August Bosio, S.D.B., the superior of the Shrine, who through all these years remained an important family friend.

Another very positive influence in Gene's life was his grandparents. His maternal grandparents, James and Catherine Burns, lived with the family for a number of years until their deaths.

His paternal grandparents, James and Elizabeth Hamilton, lived in Haverstraw and were also an important part of their grandchildren's lives. To this day people recall that Gene was particularly kind to his grandparents.

He writes in his autobiography: "My mother showed me what true love and perseverance were by caring for my grandparents in our home. Such an experience gave me time to spend with them in their final years, treasuring their words with the wisdom of many years on this earth. They embraced their illnesses knowing that it was all part of God's plan for them. They taught my brother and me the importance of family, as well as the grace that is given to those who suffer and those who care for them."[2]

A powerful influence of another kind came into Gene's life — this was the example of two fine, dedicated priests who were burdened with illness, and in both cases with partial blindness. The experiences of these two priests were a counterpoint to the faith and fun provided at the Marian Shrine. Early in life Gene was to learn that to be a good Christian requires patience and perseverance in the face of serious illness. Father Peter Malet, the assistant at the parish, was an enthusiastic and deeply dedicated man, despite a severe case

Gene after a swim during the summer at the Marian Shrine.

of diabetes, which took his life when he was only thirty-nine years old. Gene described him as "a priest who served, who suffered, and who loved."

There was also an elderly Filipino priest, Father Pastor Rafer, who came to Haverstraw as an exile because of his outspoken criticism of the Marcos regime. Later Gene would write: "His rock-like faith and enthusiasm about doing God's Will were evident in all that he did. . . . Both Father Peter and Father Rafer had poor eyesight, yet both were able to see Christ in others."[3] As an altar boy, Gene had to help the older priest, blinded by illness, around the sanctuary as he celebrated the Mass from memory.

Not all the priests in Gene's life were ill. He writes glowingly of his relationship with Father Gabriel La Paz, who served the Latin community and who introduced him to the role of an altar boy, and remained a friend for life.

Being an altar boy is an introduction for many priests to their vocation (including myself), but I have seldom seen this service described in such an enthusiastic way:

> My eight years as an altar boy fostered in me a
> devotion to Christ's Presence in the Eucharist, a
> deeper understanding of death and resurrection

Gene with his maternal grandparents, James and Catherine Burns, at his eighth-grade graduation.

through serving funerals, and a respect for the love two people proclaim to each other before God in the Sacrament of Matrimony. And so it was Father Gabriel who, along with Father Peter, provided me with examples of the essence of the priesthood.[4]

When Gene was in the fourth grade, his father's ordination to the diaconate would make a great impression on him. He writes in his autobiography:

The various installations preceding ordination made me realize the power and wonder of God. It also highlighted the fact that the bishop, priest, and deacon are vehicles through which the grace of God flows. As ministers of the Sacraments, which are ways in which Christ comes to His people, the spiritual nature and mission of Christ's bishops, priests, and deacons became clear to me. I have been fortunate in being able to see the various ways in which my father serves the community and in so doing serves Christ. Bringing Viaticum to the dying, baptizing children, witnessing marriages, and presiding at wake services introduced me in an even fuller way to the services performed by the Church's ordained ministers.

He mentioned also that his father, as a good deacon, assisted people in their physical and temporal needs, and says that this helped him to have a deeper understanding of men.[5]

The album of family photographs contains a beautiful one of Cardinal Cooke embracing the family at the time of Gene's father's ordination to the diaconate. Many years later it would strike Gene that the hand of the Cardinal rests on his shoulder just above the spot where his fatal tumor would later occur.

The family photographs that accompany this chapter show

an enthusiastic, bright-eyed, and handsome youngster being confirmed, graduating from school, embracing his grandparents. One would have thought that these pictures anticipated a beautiful and long life of service and dedication as a good Christian man, and perhaps as a priest.

At Albertus Magnus High School

In September of 1986 Gene was enrolled in Albertus Magnus High School in Bardonia, New York. This is a coed Catholic high school with a friendly atmosphere and an obviously strong religious orientation. In high school it is common enough for a student to be identified as a "future leader." This is a vague designation and usually conveys the picture of an outgoing personality, with a fair amount of ability and qualities of decency. In most cases this future leader is someone who is honest and cares about the rights and needs of others. Gene Hamilton was all of these things, but he was also a person with a significant spiritual dimension. He was openly religious, actively led and participated in religious activities, and not only spoke of the qualities of Christian discipleship, but clearly and consistently tried to live them himself. In his world of parish, CYO, and Catholic high school activities, it is no surprise that many said, "He will be a priest." His own notes and his description of himself as a private person suggest that he was not aware of this common assessment of himself by many who knew him well.

Latin Honor Society members at Albertus Magnus High School — Dawn Patton and Gene.

A Special Friend

Our best glimpse of him as a high school student comes

from Sister Miriam Joseph Schaub, a Dominican sister of Sparkill, who was his Latin and religion teacher during his high school years. In a letter written after his death she reveals a great deal in a few lines:

> From the beginning there was a bond between Gene and me, and I always felt he was too good for this world. Gene was an excellent student, yet humble and modest about his many accomplishments. He always went the extra mile and did the extra assignments. I always called on him to do the hardest part of the daily translation, and sent him to the board for the most difficult sentence to put into Latin, so that the other students would know with certainty why Gene got such good marks in my class. Gene never failed to make me proud of him.
>
> Whenever a student wanted to see Gene's homework, he always found time during the day to teach that student what was not clear about a particular problem, and he did this unobtrusively. Gene was well liked by all his teachers, and by the fellows and girls in his class.[6]

Although Gene did not speak to many people about being a priest, he seems to have made this very clear to Sister Miriam Joseph. She recalls that he frequently spoke about the great desire he had to be a priest. She writes: "I used to encourage him to attend Mass as often as possible, to spend time with Our Lord in the Blessed Sacrament, to pray the Rosary, to read the Scripture, to practice living in the presence of God, and to do everything out of love of God. I believe that Gene saw God in everyone and everything that happened to him."[7] It is not surprising then that Gene was invited to give a beautiful presentation marking the retirement of Sister Miriam Joseph and the completion of fifty-five years of teaching.

Sister Miriam Joseph, although getting on in years herself, managed to make it to Sloan-Kettering and Good Samaritan Hospital when Gene was ill. Their conversations were revealing:

> He always was so full of hope that he would be cured of cancer through the intercession of Cardinal Cooke, whom he loved and admired. I never saw Gene any other way but calm, patient, and full of faith, hope, and love, and most cooperative with the doctors and nurses. They were so edified by his sincerity and cooperation. I never heard him complain about pain and weakness.[8]

Even though he was seriously ill himself, Gene would go to the motherhouse of the Dominicans in Sparkill to visit Sister Miriam Joseph after her retirement. One day while there he visited a Sister Susan, who was dying of cancer. "He sat beside her bed, took her hand, and spoke to her about God's love for her, and how much grace she was receiving to respond to that love even in suffering. He was dressed in his black suit, and I thought to myself, 'There's Father Gene in action already.' " Later, in December of 1996, a month before his death, Gene told Sister Miriam Joseph that he was still filled with hope that he would be a priest.

While Sister Miriam Joseph cannot be accused of being overly objective or critical in her evaluation of her favorite student, at least hear her words. Obviously these were motivated by someone who was very close, but I feel it would be remiss not to put her words into this biography: "When I heard the news of Gene's death, I felt I had the privilege of personally knowing a saint. When I heard the news of his ordination on his deathbed, I was positive that Father Gene Hamilton is a saint and a priest forever!"[9]

The Lessons of Pain and Prayer

One of the things that Sister's letter does not bring out is that Eugene's years in high school were also marked by illness. Early in high school he developed extremely severe back pain. This remained undiagnosed throughout his life. It was so severe that it was necessary for him to receive the Tenz treatment. This is a device which is attached to the back of the patient with adhesive and administers an electrical current that interferes with the experience of pain. Throughout his high-school years and much of college Eugene suffered from this extreme pain that made it impossible for him to be involved in any athletic activities. Nevertheless, he was extremely busy and involved in all the other activities. Later on, recalling his four high-school years, Gene saw them as the time that he really decided to be a priest. He continued to be an altar boy after graduating from grammar school and remained so all during high school. These were the years when he was friendly with Father La Paz and Father Rafer.

He also was a leader in the Catholic Youth Organization (CYO) and described his work as being able to achieve the goal of helping other teenagers understand our faith and live it. He was at this time particularly influenced by Monsignor Raymond Powers, who, along with being pastor of St. Paul's Church in Congers, was the moderator of the CYO for Rockland County. It was Monsignor Powers whom he first told about the possibility of his calling to be a priest. Monsignor Powers responded "by telling me how much he loved being a priest. That enthusiasm was quite evident to all who ever met Monsignor Powers."[10] In his sophomore year he was selected to participate in the Hugh O'Brien Leadership Conference held at Rensselaer Polytechnic Institute.

As a serious candidate for the priesthood, Gene's life began to take on certain aspects of his future vocation. The Blessed Sacrament became very much the center of his life, especially when in his senior year he was mandated to be a eucharistic minister for his high school. He also developed at this time a strong personal devotion to St. Joseph.

As a result of his severe pain he had to withdraw from all athletics, but volunteered to be the statistician of his high school basketball team. He participated in all school activities, went to the dances and socials, and had many friends both male and female. Some must have doubted that one so outgoing and involved would go to the seminary, but his friends who were girls remember that this was exactly the relationship — they were close friends who were girls, and not girlfriends. As one might have expected, at graduation he received special recognition as salutatorian and was awarded the Latin and Social Studies medals. What Gene really wanted was to begin college as a candidate for the priesthood.

But a disappointment was waiting for him. Because of his illness and the therapy that he needed, his application to the Neumann Residence for potential seminarians was put on hold. This residence in the Riverdale section of the Bronx — founded by Cardinal Cooke — is a program where students for the priesthood live while attending various colleges in the area. Their

Gene at his high school graduation.

college courses are supplemented by philosophy and theology courses taught at the residence. They are also provided with spiritual direction and a liturgical and prayerful life. Gene writes that having his application put on hold caused him much anguish:

> After much prayer and anxiety, I felt that my illness would preclude me from entering the Neumann Residence and attending Manhattan College at the same time. Nevertheless, I also had the feeling that there was something that God wanted me to explore, experience, or understand at Manhattan [College]. I chose to go there and hopefully come closer to determining what God wanted me to do with my life.[11]

However, the edge was taken off Gene's disappointment when Monsignor James Sullivan graciously allowed him to come to Neumann for Mass whenever he could.

At Manhattan College

Gene was in residence for four years at Manhattan College, located, as Neumann is, in the upper Bronx. This college, conducted by the Christian Brothers, became an extremely important part of Gene's life. Later on, he would remember particularly that the teaching brothers would begin each class by saying, "Let us remember that we are in the presence of God." He writes: "Such an invocation had an effect upon how I viewed life and the world around me. Recognizing the presence of God in my everyday life also led me to realize where God's presence was lacking. While observing the struggles between good and evil, I also marveled at other people's search for God. Despite our shortcomings and failings, a large majority of my peers were searching for that which will bring them peace and salvation. This desire to know and love God on the part of others encouraged me."[12]

Gene soon became involved in the Office of Campus Ministry of the college and was liturgical coordinator of the eucharistic ministers. Eventually he was also put in charge of the sacristy, where, among other things, he coordinated the requests of students and alumni who wished to celebrate the Sacrament of Matrimony in their college chapel. While at Manhattan he received the Branigan research fellowship, which gave him the opportunity to do an intense study of St. Thomas Aquinas, his moral philosophy, and its application to higher education. He writes: "Aquinas' life and search for God were not merely intellectual, but rather Thomas undertook a lifelong search for the Divine Presence that encompassed his whole person. Such an integration of a person's search for union with God is awe-inspiring."[13]

Gene considered it a very special blessing that he was given the opportunity to live at St. Joseph's Seminary for one whole summer, from May to July, so that he could have the opportunity to do the research called for by the Branigan Research Fellowship. Monsignor Powers welcomed him to Dunwoodie, and Gene writes: "I spent many a night not just in the library but also in the chapel and on the outside grounds. The peculiar aspect of that summer experience in the seminary was the silence. It was the silence that forced me to listen harder. It was the silence that made me examine why I felt God was calling me to the priesthood. It was the silence that allowed me to struggle with my doubts and fears. And it was in the silence that I asked Jesus for guidance and direction. I left the Seminary with the desire to serve Christ through others during the next two years of college, while also coming to the inevitable conclusion of renewing my application for admission to the Neumann Residence."[14]

During his senior year at Manhattan, Gene was elected president of the student government, in which he had been active all four years. He wrote that: "My current position as President presents me with an opportunity to serve the student body. . . . There is an obligation to be a witness to the Catholic faith as well. . . ."[15]

The faculty and staff of Manhattan College realized that they had an outstanding man on their hands. In the very impressive brochure of the college, Eugene's picture was featured and his statement on the challenge of Catholic education is given. To someone reading this biography, it is also obvious that this statement is edited, a piece of public relations, because it does not directly mention the spiritual aspects of Catholic higher education. Perhaps Gene's view of things was a bit too much for the people in charge of public relations, who were trying to influence less spiritually oriented candidates.

In writing his application for the Neumann Residence, Gene revealed much about his own inner dynamics. Three concepts stand out clearly in reviewing this material. One is the presence of God who calls us; the second is the freedom that we have to choose whether we will answer that call or not; and third is Eugene's view of the priesthood.

The Call of God

> What happens to us in Providence is in all essential respects what His voice was to those whom He addressed when on earth: whether He commands us by a visible presence, or by a voice, or by our consciences, it matters not, so that we feel it to be a command. If it is a command, it may be obeyed or disobeyed; it may be accepted as Samuel or St. Paul accepted it, or put aside after the manner of the young man who had great possessions.
>
> *Venerable John Henry Newman*[16]

In his four years at Manhattan College the meaning of the call of God began to develop — as it must do if this call is to grow and become a vocation. To borrow the words of St. Augustine, Gene came to know that he had not chosen the Way, but that the Way had chosen him. Viewed from a purely rationalistic perspective — a call to the priesthood is simply a process of career selection, and indeed there are certain similarities between a call and a career. But describing a call to the priesthood or any other life of discipleship as a "career" seems to be the equivalent of describing St. Paul as a discontented Jewish scholar or Michelangelo's Sistine Chapel as a painted hall. Experience has shown that reducing the priesthood, or any other Christian vocation, to such flat, two-dimensional terms is debilitating to faith and undermines the very life of the Church. A quarter of a century of work as a psychologist evaluating vocations has convinced me that a purely rationalistic attitude toward the priesthood is responsible for the shortage of priests and for the loss of many vocations in the past decades. In our discussions, to be faithful to Gene's own words, we have to accept a vocation as a call from God and not simply a career. Those who think of the priesthood as a career, or simply as a function, will never understand Eugene Hamilton, and in fact will be disturbed by the very mysterious fulfillment of his vocation.

Fortunately, Eugene himself has left us a moving and well-articulated description of his vocation which, though incomplete, accounts for the extraordinary way in which he dealt with the last months and weeks of his short life.

This account is in the form of an outline of a book that he apparently began writing after his final diagnosis of terminal cancer and the realization that Memorial Sloan Kettering Hospital could offer no new treatment. The shocking news that the staff could do no more was delivered to him on June 20, 1996. Gene notes that this is the eve of the memorial of St. Aloysius Gonzaga, a Jesuit seminarian who on that very day died while caring for plague victims in Rome. The saint was in his early twenties when he died.

From Gene's writings it is not possible to trace the time sequence of his developing vocational ideas — rather, we can read of his deep spirituality of the priesthood and relate it to events at Manhattan and after his graduation. By gathering incidents here and there which illustrate his well-articulated and in many ways profound ideals of the priesthood, we can construct what may be called the story of a soul.

The Most Significant Influence — The Call to the Priesthood

It is very clear from his autobiography that Gene saw the vocation to be a priest both as a call from God and as a completely voluntary response.

> Throughout my life, due to a variety of experiences, I have slowly grown to rely on God and seek His Will. My free will consists in choosing Him Who placed me on this earth for a reason. The reason I am entering the Neumann Residence is to determine whether God is indeed calling me to the priesthood, or perhaps it is to remind myself that God has already been calling me to the priesthood. He did not provide me with a lightning bolt (although at times it would have made this journey easier); rather He provided me with a consistent, constant "knowing." No voices, no revelations. Yes, the events of my life provide me with some signs — the suggestions of others to examine the possibility of a vocation to the priesthood, the calling of God through Scripture, the awareness of Jesus working within human history and specifically within my own life. Now it is time to see whether Christ is calling me, through the Church, to serve Him as a priest. Would I make a good Catholic husband and father in a day and age when Christian marriage and family life are deteriorating from various perspectives? I hope and I pray that I would. Would I make a good Catholic attorney or leader of another sort, who would remain true to his principles and beliefs, in a world

that seems valueless? I hope and pray that I would. Would I make a good priest? I hope so, but it is an awesome challenge.[17]

Gene was not someone to borrow a phrase or even to sincerely use the words of another to account for what he was doing. He was intent on making even well-defined concepts like the priesthood his own when he used them. In the following page from the autobiography, he uses traditional phraseology, and in fact ideas which are not popular today — but he does not simply repeat them, he makes them his own:

The priest is an *alter Christus*, another Christ. Our Lord calls individuals to the priesthood; it is determined by our free will whether we answer in the affirmative. What does it mean to "be" Christ? The priest must remember the basic mission of Jesus: redemption and salvation. Thus the basic mission of a priest is a spiritual one. The priest is called to intercede between God and His people. He does this by witnessing the love that brings man and woman together in the Sacrament of Marriage. He does this by being an example of the love of God when welcoming a new member into the family of God through Baptism. He does this by bringing Christ Himself to others through the Eucharist and the comfort of Christ to others through the Anointing of the Sick. He does this by being the vehicle through which Christ forgives our sins and provides us with the graces to lead good Christian lives in the Sacrament of Reconciliation. The priest assists his bishop, a successor of the Apostles, in the Sacrament of Confirmation, in calling down the Holy Spirit upon God's people. The priest witnesses the spiritual begetting of other priests on the part of his bishop in the Sacrament of Holy Orders. Thus the priest must be one who loves and can bring the love that Christ has to others.[18]

This beautiful and succinct description of the life and work of a priest, focused on the sacraments — not as simple rituals but rather as vital encounters with Christ — should elicit a deeply felt "Yes" from any priest or seminarian. Even those jaded by rationalistic and superficial concepts of the priesthood can hardly fail to be attracted by this deeply Christ-centered ideal. Here the priest is described not simply as a functionary, not even simply as an evangelizer (as much as that is part of the priesthood), but rather as a man set apart by God and sent to give the means of salvation in the name and person of Christ. How did this young man, so vitally involved in the atmosphere of his school, so obviously part of the culture in which he lived — although selectively — how did he come by such an ideal, personal, spiritual, traditional, and even, in the proper sense of the term, mystical?

The answer to this question is simply to be found in one place, a powerful Christ-centered place, used in the most pervasive and revealing way by Christians from St. Paul to the martyrs of the twentieth century — in the Cross of Jesus Christ. Remember when you read these and the following words that they were written from the heart by a fine and vibrant young man at the end of the twentieth century, certain that the priest is called to love and to bring the love of Christ to others. Gene wrote:

> The greatest manifestation of the love of Christ was seen when He spread His arms on the Cross. Thus the priest must take up his cross like Christ, and must suffer like Christ. He must conform his will to that of the Father like Christ, and he must

"be" Christ. The essence of the priesthood is the Cross. As humans we tend to think of the mortality of the Cross; the priest must realize the immortality of the Cross. The priest must realize that suffering turns into redemption, that love overcomes death, that salvation is found in that act of holy sacrifice known as the Mass. The constant meditation upon the Cross of Christ symbolizes the ministry of the priest. For the priest his place is in the world, but he is not to be of the world. That is the challenge facing those who receive the Sacrament of Holy Orders. It is a challenge that takes place within the spiritual and human realms every day. It is a challenge that brings joy to those who serve Him as priests.[19]

What Is a Priest in the Catholic Church?

Since the goal of the priesthood shaped the life of Gene it is necessary to pause and to consider what indeed is the ideal that directed his entire life. During the past several decades there has been a tendency to see the priesthood as many things which are not expressed in Gene's ideal. Some of these are in fact very good things. A priest, like a Protestant minister, can be a pastoral counselor, a healer of the soul, an agent of community action and of witness against injustice; a priest can be a teacher, a scholar, an administrator. None of these things I have mentioned are inimical to the priesthood in any way, but they are not the core of the Catholic priesthood any more than older roles like patriarch of the immigrant village or spokesman for the oppressed were the core of the priesthood in nineteenth-century America.

My own experience in speaking to many who have given up a priestly vocation is that the core of the priesthood, so profoundly expressed in the insight of this college student, was missing or had been lost, or at least partially undermined by rationalistic ideas of this call as a career, or worse yet, merely a function.

At times the priesthood has been bolstered up in our own confused culture by other deeply religious ideals, spiritually consistent with it, but offering another dimension. The importance of the contemplative ideal expressed by Thomas Merton in *The Seven Storey Mountain* illustrated that the priestly vocation could be an expression of monastic spirituality. Outstanding priests with complex spiritual identities have actually brought vitality to the lived Catholic priesthood in modern times. Whether it is an ideal of an order and its founder, like St. Maximilian Kolbe the conventual Franciscan, or the input of scholars who are priests — a Jesuit like de Lubac, or a diocesan priest like Von Balthasar — they were men who brought to the priesthood something else, something consistent, and yet beyond the simple ideal of the priesthood.

To Bring Christ in His Own Person

The simple and essential statement of the vocation of the priest is that he is to bring Christ to the people of God, especially with and through the sacraments and pastoral ministry, because he is conformed to Christ by his priestly ordination. This ideal has been overlooked and at times indirectly disparaged. It may be acceptable and really helpful for someone to be a hyphenated priest — a priest-teacher, a priest-administrator, a priest-psychologist, a priest-scientist — but the core of the vocation is a mysterious identity of the individual priest with Christ as shepherd of the flock of God.

A thorough examination of Gene's writing and discussions with his family and friends reveals that he was always motivated by the simple and unqualified ideal of the Catholic priesthood. Although he admired the Salesians who guided his youth, and had a special devotion to Redemptorist St. John Neumann, he showed no inclination to join a religious community. He was attracted to no special work as a priest. His example should be a source of encouragement, especially to diocesan seminarians and priests, because the rich spirituality of the priesthood was simply the same priestly spirituality which has been so powerfully advocated by Pope John Paul II. It is not too much to say that this pope embodies the spiritual identity of the priest more than anyone else in modern public life.

From the very beginning of his pontificate, Pope John Paul II has worked to rebuild the spiritual identity of the Catholic priesthood eroded by rationalism, by superficiality, and by a tendency to reduce the priesthood to a mere function. From his letter to bishops and priests for Holy Thursday, 1979, in the first year of his pontificate, to the Apostolic Exhortatoin, *Pastores Dabo Vobis*, he has reiterated the simple but profound truth that the priest is called to serve and minister to the faithful in the name of Christ, and to conform himself to the person of Christ the Good Shepherd by prayer, toil, generous service, and the suffering that may be required to do this. It is a para-

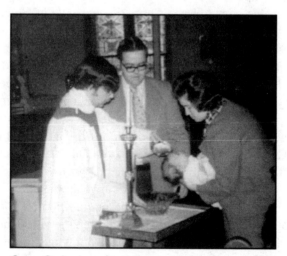

Gene Sr. looks on as Margaret holds baby Gene at his baptism.

dox of history that never in modern times has there been such a consistent exposition of the meaning of the priesthood by a pope and at the same time such a loss of identity, such confusion of roles, and such a subtle rejection of the mystery and supernatural origin of the priesthood and its essential task of shepherding the people of God in the place of Christ. It must be borne in mind that Eugene and many other young aspirants to the priesthood at the present seek to embrace this identity when there is confusion, scandal, and even when theologians who are themselves priests present the Sacrament of Holy Orders and its meaning in a way that not only departs from the Catholic tradition, but even calls into question the dogmatic teaching of their own Church.

The origins of Gene's clear, deeply spiritual, and yet very humane ideal of the priesthood are not difficult to identify. He was profoundly impressed with the spirituality of Terence Cardinal Cooke. As we go further in this study we shall explore this influence and see how it became central in the last months of Gene's life. The priests who gave support and formation to Gene were men who obviously loved and cherished a clear commitment to the Catholic priesthood. His own family was imbued with an unequivocal and vibrant faith. Of course his experience in college and the atmosphere of pervasive theological confusion and conflict that characterizes our time made him more aware that not all people accepted his ideal of the priesthood. But Gene was fortunate enough to live at a time when the few who seek a vocation to the priesthood seem to have developed an immunity from confusion and the inroads of rationalism all around them.

Endnotes

1. Autobiography, 4. This document will be referred to simply as "Autobiography" and the original pagination will be used.
2. Ibid., 4.

3. Ibid., 5-6.

4. Ibid., 3.

5. Ibid., 3-4.

6. Letter of Sister Miriam Joseph Schaab, O.P., to author.

7. Ibid.

8. Ibid.

9. Ibid.

10. Autobiography, 6-7.

11. Ibid., 7.

12. Ibid., 8.

13. Ibid., 9.

14. Ibid., 9-10.

15. Ibid., 10.

16. *Parochial and Plain Sermons*, volume 8, sermon 2, "Divine Calls," excerpted in *The Heart of Newman*, Erich Przywara, S.J., ed. San Francisco: Ignatius Press, 1997, p. 227.

17. Autobiography, 11.

18. Ibid., 11-12.

19. Ibid., 12-13.

2.

College Student and Disciple

Gene and Brother
Thomas Scanlan

Although a number of commuter students attend Manhattan College, Gene lived there and was very much part of the college life. It could have been an anomalous situation.

He could have simply stepped back, confined his activities to the chapel, and spent much of his time at Neumann, where he was always welcomed by the rector, the faculty, and the students. But his own ideal of the priesthood, his self-concept that a Christian is to be a leaven in human society, pushed him more and more into the life of the college. It was not difficult to see that Gene's years at Manhattan, though not his preference, were a providential part of his life. Even without Holy Orders, it is not too much to say that he was a disciple or perhaps even an apostle on the campus.

When one reads the remembrances, the accomplishments, and the evaluations of Gene's teachers and fellow students at Manhattan College, the words "outstanding" and "remarkable" come to mind. Although suffering with a pain serious enough to deter his entrance into Neumann, Gene managed to accomplish a great many things, mostly for other people. In no way did his already deep spirituality keep him from being a vital part of college life. Gene, who had been active in the pro-life movement in the CYO, brought his strong convictions on this crucial issue to Manhattan. He was able to breathe some new life into the movement at the college by emphasizing the moral and spiritual aspects of pro-life activism, rather than focusing on the political approach. His interest in the pro-life cause would, of course, take a new turn when he became terminally ill. His parents report that he saw facing his terminal condition as very consciously a witness against euthanasia, a subject that was much in the media at that time.

Along with being a volunteer sacristan and eucharistic minister, he was engaged in a rather elaborate student government that offered an experience of public life and service that most college presidents would envy. He served on the senate and as a judge, but also as a volunteer aide to assist students who had partied too much on Friday nights. As we might expect, we get different pictures of him from those who knew him in different ways.

Dean Mary Ann O'Donnell saw Gene in her role as an administrator. He seemed to be a budding professional, but also managed to be a friend:

> My recollections of Gene Hamilton are many and varied, partly because Gene and I worked very closely on developing a new governance system for Manhattan College, including a restructured

College Senate and a redeveloped committee system. Gene was a brilliant strategist, one who read opposing views well and knew when and how to compromise to get those in opposing camps to get to some reasonable agreement that did not sell out the principles we worked to uphold, namely full participation of all with subsidiarity paramount. . . .

While he and I did not agree about some major issues of religion and Church life, he never tried to proselytize me or show me how wrong I was. Since he respected our differences of opinion (as I did also), we could discuss openly these differences.[1]

In a rather revealing note she adds: "Gene did not suffer fools gladly, but he was never unkind. When someone was being obstinate, idiotic, or just plain stupid, he did not castigate, but he also did not make excuses for that person or accept inappropriate behavior."[2]

In the eulogy that she gave for Eugene in the student senate on February 19, 1997, Dr. O'Donnell remembered a number of interesting details:

My best memories of Gene are from Senate and Governance meetings, and of his moving between stubborn and uncompromising groups. Gene would be in jacket and tie, looking more professorial than we the professors did, and he taught us. He taught us that compromise was not a loss, that all could win if we listened to one another and sought understanding. I can still see him coming into my office to say, "Dean, what if . . . ." and what followed would be brilliant in its simplicity and clarity.

What many did not know of Gene back then is

that he was in great pain — even then — from an unusual condition that struck him while he was in high school. . . . He slept little, but he used those hours in the dark night NOT to curse the pain but to read, reflect, pray, and to hammer out drafts and redrafts of the new Senate constitution, the very Constitution we are governed by today.

Two weeks before he died, we spoke about the pain he was in as a student and of the pain he was in that day. I could hear the smile in his voice as he told me that the pain he experienced in college was good training for the pain he was experiencing that gray January day. He wasted nothing, not even his pain.[3]

It is worthwhile mentioning that Dr. O'Donnell's recollections of Gene very much echo those of Sister Miriam Joseph when she wrote about his high school years. Both of these

At the Honors Ceremony in May, 1994, Gene received the Joseph Gunn Medal, the most distinguished award given at graduation. At left is Brother Thomas Scanlan, president of Manhattan College; Deacon Gene Hamilton; Gene; Margaret Hamilton; and Ann Marie Burke, president of Manhattan College Alumni society.

people who knew Gene well in his academic environment expressed the hope that other students would grow because of their experience of having known so fine a young man. Dr. O'Donnell in her eulogy said the following:

> All of us who worked in Senate, in student government, in judiciary, all of us knew that we were working with a unique person, someone very special. We know even more so now. It is my hope, my petition, my prayer that those of us who worked with Senator Eugene Hamilton (as well as those who will learn about him in the future) will derive from him new strength to persevere, to chart the right course, to work tirelessly for the common good, to make Manhattan a better place.[4]

Gene was particularly interested in philosophy and was a delight to any professor of the subject, which a good many students avoid or are even unaware of. Dr. Rentaro Hashimoto, the chairman of the department of philosophy at Manhattan, provides us with a teacher's view of this remarkable student:

> Gene was in many respects everything a teacher looks for in a student: intelligent, sensitive, articulate, literate, industrious, and politically and socially conscious. Broadly humanistic in his interests, he had a fund of general knowledge unusual in any age, but particularly now when the average student shows little inclination toward or respect for the life of the mind. In addition to majoring in philosophy, he minored in history, government, and religious studies.
> When I first met him, I was struck above all by his poise and articulateness. This was a young man who could speak in complete, grammatically

correct sentences without stumbling over his words. As a freshman, he was obviously quite traditional both by training and inclination. It was gratifying to see him gradually overcome his somewhat strait-laced habits and mature into the warm, tolerant, and magnanimous person he became. I was particularly happy to see his sense of humor develop to the point that we could laugh at the same things. I still recall his infectious giggle. . . .

He was also quietly and unobtrusively solicitous of the well-being of his fellow students. He volunteered in a group called Campus Watch that directed intoxicated students from the local bars back to their dorms.

His conscientiousness as Student Government President was also displayed when he rushed back to school one weekend from his home in Rockland County to help the victims of a fire in Jasper Hall. Thanks to his efforts several students displaced by the fire were soon placed in other accommodations.

I was aware that he suffered increasingly from chronic health problems that affected his breathing and caused him intense back pain. Often he had to leave class because sitting for long periods aggravated his back problem. As a result he was able to sleep only fitfully because he was never without pain. Despite this he never looked disgruntled, dyspeptic, or out of sorts. This was perhaps his outstanding quality. His equanimity was almost preternatural, based in large part on his solid Christian faith and a happy stoical temperament. He never complained, not, I believe, even unconsciously.[5]

College Student and Disciple

In a final note to Gene, Professor Hashimoto cited Psalm 46, "God is our refuge and our strength, an ever present help in trouble" (vs. 1). Then he wrote these most complimentary lines, which must have embarrassed the dying young student:

> I pray for you daily. I hope these passages from the Psalms are of some comfort to you. After all sorts of twisting and turning I've fully accepted that Christ's love is expressed through suffering, physical or spiritual. This is the testimony of St. Paul, St. Augustine, Simone Weil and now you.
>
> In William James' *Varieties of Religious Experience* that I'm using this time around in Philosophy of Religion, there's a description of you: "Some persons are born with an inner constitution which is harmonious and well balanced from the outset." Further, "their impulses are consistent with one another, their will follows without trouble the guidance of their intellect, their passions are not excessive, and their lives are little haunted by regrets." Do you recognize yourself in these words?[6]

It may be difficult for the reader who did not know Gene personally to grasp the unusual impact that he had on those who knew him. It is easy enough to assume (but erroneous in this case) that death may have subtly put a halo around a young person with many positive traits. How do we communicate that he was really quite exceptional apart from any mystique which may have come from his untimely death?

Dr. John Wilcox, the chairman of the Religious Studies Department at Manhattan, recalls that at a meeting on ethics and values, one of the faculty at Mt. St. Vincent, a neighboring college in the Bronx, asked who the new faculty member was. At that time Gene could not have been more than twenty-one years old. In a public reminiscence about Gene Dr. Wilcox said:

> I think of St. Thérèse of Lisieux, the young Carmelite nun whose age was the same as Gene's when she died in 1897. She said she would spend eternity showering God's grace on us all. I don't think it unfounded to believe that Gene is doing the same for all those who shared his life as a Jasper [a local term for a student] or who carry on the traditions which he so eagerly embraced at Manhattan College.[7]

Another insight, or rather a collection of insights, is given by Gene's professor of history, Dr. Julie Leininger Pycior. She was impressed enough at the time to make very accurate notes on the baccalaureate Mass at which Gene spoke:

> At the baccalaureate Mass (on Pentecost), Gene's father served as the deacon and his brother Tom was an usher. The celebrant offered to let Gene give the homily, but Gene always was scrupulous about obeying regulations and thought that a lay person should only speak after Communion. In his remarks he said, among other things, "The Holy Spirit working through the Catholic Church, through Christ's Body, and through each of us, is waiting to consume us in the fire of love that conquers the darkness of the world, a world that has either misunderstood passion or remained passionless. Our experiences here at Manhattan prepare us for this new relationship with the Holy Spirit, this new role we are playing in this world." A few hours later, as we faculty members were assembling to process into graduation, Gene came by to say goodbye to several of us. He embraced me

unselfconsciously and whispered, "Thanks for everything."[8]

Gene had a very personal way of handling thorny issues. The following vignette of Dr. Pycior is quite illustrative of his genuinely charitable and competent way of handling difficult things:

> Then came the Pope's visit to Dunwoodie. On my next telephone call to Gene I of course knew that he would have loved to have been there and I expressed my sorrow in that regard. Because he was such a dear friend I did not stop there, however, but plunged ahead, not knowing how he would respond. I added that I couldn't be part of the crowd outside because if I had gone I would have had to hold up a placard reading "Ordain Women." Gene replied, "If I'd have been there, I would have waved to you."[9]

Interestingly, Dr. Pycior, like Dr. Wilcox, sees a similarity between Gene and St. Thérèse; this is a rather amazing thing, since these two professors wrote quite independently:

> To me Father Gene Hamilton is like St. Thérèse, as when she wrote, "I care now about one thing only — to love You, my Jesus! Great deeds are forbidden me, I cannot preach the Gospel nor shed my blood — but what does it matter? The only way I can prove my love is by . . . doing the least of actions for love. I wish both to suffer and to find joy through love." I hope that Father Eugene Hamilton's spiritual writings also can be published. It would be fitting that another *Story of a Soul* appear on the centenary of Thérèse's death.[10]

A Priest Forever

A different aspect of Gene's personality emerges when we hear about what he was to his fellow students. The hard-working, politically astute young man is now seen as someone with a great deal of tenderness and compassion. There are many stories illustrating this, but two will suffice. A young student named Colette Dolan was a very close friend of Gene and worked with him on the student government. Colette was the recipient of many of Gene's kindnesses, especially when things were not going well for her. Recently she wrote:

> Gene has gotten me through so many broken hearts, professional setbacks, and other trials and tribulations of young adult life that he always said that he was either going to send me a very large bill

Gene worked at a camera store in Haverstraw and posed for this picture on October 31, 1992, as part of his job. His smile could "light up a room," and as this picture shows, he was not a serious stick-in-the-mud!

for his counseling services or write a book about me — he assured me that it would be a best seller!

The one thing I remember most about Gene is his smile — it could light up a room. It was either a source of great comfort or made you wonder what he was up to! One occasion when I saw that smile was Valentine's Day, 1991. It fell in the midst of a very trying time for me. Over the previous months, I had lost over thirty pounds and doctor after doctor shrugged in confusion. Due to my family's track record with cancer, it was decided that I should have a biopsy. This was to occur a few days after Valentine's. I was so preoccupied and nervous about the impending procedure that I had completely forgotten about Valentine's Day. But Gene didn't. I bumped into him in the Quad and, flashing that famous smile, he suggested that I go to my car. When I got there, the driver's seat was covered with a white sheet. Underneath was a big, white teddy bear holding a dozen red roses and two cards that told me how special I was. To this day, I have no idea how he got in my car!!! At that moment, I knew I would always be OK as long as I had Gene in my life. That story is one of dozens. There was my twentieth birthday when Gene took me to see "The Phantom of the Opera" at the Elmsford Dinner Theater. After the show, he had a cake for me and the cast sang "Happy Birthday."[11]

Another event must be more delicately told. Gene's mother recalls that when he was in first-year college, Mary Holmes, one of the teachers at Albertus Magnus High School, called about a student at the school who was disappointed not to be able to go to the prom. She desperately wanted to go. But not having been asked and being short on funds this seemed impossible. Gene himself at this time was very busy in college and limited financially also. In fact, he did not know this young lady very well. Nevertheless, he invited her and was able to defray the costs, which for him were substantial. It does not take much insight to realize that this was an extraordinary act of kindness — one appreciated by the young lady and her family, but also by the very few other people, like Mary Holmes, who knew what really happened.

A student for the priesthood may feel intimidated even on the campus of a religiously sponsored college. He may come to see many of his fellow students as people wasting their talents or frittering away their time on aimless socializing and partying. Gene had a very different view. In his autobiography he writes about college:

> Recognizing the presence of God in my everyday life also led me to recognize where God's presence was lacking. While observing the struggles between good and evil, I also marveled at other people's search for God. Despite our shortcomings and failures, a large majority of my peers were searching for that which would bring them peace and salvation. This desire to know and love God on the part of others encourage me.[12]

Gene mentions in several places in his notes his gratitude to his parents for providing not only an excellent home but also a very good Catholic education. He treasured this education, and in an interesting way drew out the positive elements while aware that there were many shortcomings. He valued and cherished whatever he received: "The beauty of receiving a Catholic education, which I have been grateful for all my life, is that one is able to combine the heartfelt search for God with the intellectual pursuit of the Divine as well."[13]

College Student and Disciple

Although one suspects that none of those involved in the very well-developed student government at Manhattan College realized it, Gene's participation was seen by himself in apostolic terms. For him student government was a way to evangelize. This would have been resented if it had been known — but he was subtle enough to keep it to himself. He writes in his autobiography, which was the first part of his application to the Neumann Residence, as follows:

> My time in the Senate allowed me to interact with faculty and administrators in hopes of bettering the College. My tenure as Chief Justice of the Student Court taught me the dual importance of justice and mercy. My current position as President of Student Government presents me with an opportunity to serve the student body. Being a Student Government President at a Catholic college provides an added dimension to the position. There is an obligation to be a witness to the Catholic

Gene is a lector at his graduation Mass from the St. John Neumann Residence, May, 1995.

faith as well as remain true to the mission of the institution. Such a struggle is becoming even more pronounced on campuses across the country. Catholic higher education is at a crossroads, where the Seekers of Truth must once again meet Him Who is the Truth. The dynamics of the Catholic Church are that it is a divine institution comprised of human beings. It is a means through which the People of God are drawn closer to Him. It is a reminder to this world that there is something more than just this world. Thus the Church's role vis-á-vis higher education needs to be examined critically and promoted consistently. I hope I met that challenge as President of Student Government at Manhattan College.[14]

Gene graduated from Manhattan in May 1994, and was honored as an outstanding student. He was invited to give the sermon art the baccalaureate Mass, but he refused. Instead, he insisted on delivering, as is proper, a post-Communion reflection at the end of Mass. It is significant, for others previously had given the talk in the place of the sermon. Gene knew that he was not authorized to give a sermon, but he actually gave a magnificent one. The talk is splendid and is included as "Addendum One."

Many thought that Gene would pursue a career in law or some other profession. Even those with strong religious values wondered if the embattled priesthood was the most effective way for such a multi-faceted personality to have a Christian effect on society. There was no question for Gene. He looked forward to a summer with his family, an interesting temporary job doing the computer work that he loved, and beginning the pre-theology program at the Neumann Residence.

Endnotes

1. Letter of Mary Ann O'Donnell to author, April 1, 1997.
2. Ibid.
3. M.A. O'Donnell, Eulogy at Manhattan College Senate meeting, February 19, 1997.
4. Ibid.
5. Letter of Dr. Rentaro Hashimoto to author, March 20, 1997.
6. Ibid.
7. Tribute of Dr. John Wilcox.
8. Julie Leininger Pycior, "Reverend Eugene R. Hamilton: Some Personal Reflections."
9. Ibid.
10. Ibid.
11. Letter of Colette Dolan to author, March 17, 1997.
12. Autobiography, 8.
13. Ibid., 8-9.
14. Ibid., 10.

The Road Toward the Priesthood

The Neumann Residence — A Place to Grow

Gene and (then)
Bishop O'Brien

Despite his strong background in philosophy and religious studies, the formation program of the archdiocese required Gene to spend a year, a very productive year, at the Neumann Residence. As we have seen, he was already very familiar with Neumann. During many visits in the four years of college he had met with Monsignor James Sullivan, the rector, who writes of him:

It was evident to me that he had a mature sense

of the call to the priesthood and that it was to be
his unique way to attain the holiness which the
Lord had willed for him. Illness and suffering were
never far from Eugene's sense of the call to holiness. . . .[1]

Indeed, illness and suffering followed Eugene to Neumann.
During the first semester he came down with a serious respira-
tory infection that caused him to miss much school. Monsignor Sullivan writes: "We were concerned that he would have
fallen behind in his academic work but Eugene returned to
master it all."[2]

During the year at Neumann, Gene was required to write a
self-evaluation. As one might expect, this document is much
more formal than his autobiography or the outline of his incomplete book. But despite the rather formal "parade dress"
approach that such a study requires, we are able to get some
real glimpses of Gene's self-image at this time.

For instance, in responding to a question on celibacy and
its implications for the seminarian and the priest, Gene writes:

The same spirit of love that motivates the pursuit of a vocation to priesthood allows me to realize the importance of celibacy and self-giving. My
relationships with women and men are varied. They
have provided me with opportunities to love within
the context of particular situations. Those same
relationships have presented me with the opportunity to discuss my own personal reflections on
celibacy in a supportive yet constructively critical
context. Realizing that chastity is a particular vocation I have been called to as a single man through
this point of my life, I feel I have remained faithful to that call. God now seems to be calling me to
make the promise of celibacy a continuation of

that original call to chastity. This call to celibacy would be rooted in an intense relationship with Jesus, His mother Mary, and His Church.[3]

Something even more revealing was found by Gene's father among his personal effects after his death. One hesitates to publish something this personal, and yet it shines a bright light on the life of our subject and an area of greatest importance at the present time. In an age of self-indulgence when many think Christ's call to celibacy is an impossible ideal, some question the usefulness and even the propriety of this requirement of the Church. If you have come to appreciate Gene Hamilton, I take responsibility, then, with his parents for sharing this very private document with you. Monsignor John Farley, spiritual director of St. Joseph's Seminary, recalls the discussions he had with Gene that led to his making this commitment. Although this vow was actually made and signed a few months before his death, it follows logically from the statement given above and it prepares in a mysterious way for what was to transpire on the last day of Gene's life, when this commitment would have to have been required if he had been able to make it before receiving the diaconate:

> I, Eugene R. Hamilton, Jr., do hereby make this private vow of celibacy on November 21, 1996, the Memorial of the Presentation of the Blessed Virgin Mary.
>
> I do so in the presence of the angels and the saints, placing the question of my vocation, ordination, and priesthood under the protection of Mary, Mother of the Church and Mother of Priests; and placing myself under the guidance and care of St. Joseph, Patron and Protector of the Universal Church and Patron of a Happy Death.
>
> I ask for the help of my guardian angel and my

patron saints in remaining faithful to this promise. I make this vow so as to grow closer to Jesus
Christ the High Priest, so that I might continue to
do the Will of the Father, and always be strength-
ened by the Holy Spirit. Amen.

Another aspect of Eugene's spiritual development during
his year at Neumann becomes clear when he writes about
prayer:

The importance of prayer to me is rooted in
my upbringing and life experiences.

Chief among these is the Holy Sacrifice of the
Mass. It is from the Eucharist that my daily prayer
takes root. Praying the Liturgy of the Hours for
me is an extension of that high point of prayer, the
Mass. From such an appreciation comes a better
understanding of Christ's Presence in the other
Sacraments as well, especially Penance. The Rosary provides an opportunity to meditate on the
mysteries of Christ's life, while walking in faith
with Mary. . . .

Thus my personal prayer life has been developed with the goal of union with God, recognizing that I have been called to serve Him and His
Church. My prayers motivate my thoughts, words,
and deeds towards this end. . . .

Intellectual examination of the importance of
honesty, chastity, docility, humility, charity, and
prudence has translated into the application of such
virtues in my everyday life. All of this takes place
while being grounded in prayer.

The ability to give Christian witness, especially
in the area of perseverance and quiet charity, is
something which stems from my trust in God.

> The listening that takes place in my spiritual life allows me to listen to other residents and provide them with whatever assistance I can.[4]

The personality of Eugene Hamilton is an interesting blend of the quiet person who knows many people and is very involved in many things. The apparent oxymoron, a quiet extrovert, seems to describe him well. He also shows little or none of the self-rejection that is one of the struggles of many people on the spiritual journey. Devout Christians as diverse as St. Francis and St. Alphonsus Liguori, Venerable Matt Talbot, and Blessed Edith Stein, have struggled quietly with self-hate, and have sought to transform it in humility. Anyone personally familiar with this subject knows that self-hate is not humility at all. It has to be baptized and ever kept at bay. One does meet people on the spiritual road who are not troubled by self-hate. They are capable of a direct look at their own personalities and seem to be able to make an accurate appraisal without either vanity or smugness. Such a person was Eugene's model, Cardinal Cooke. Humility and even a certain self-effacement was there, but after much studying of him and his life I could not find any self-hate when I wrote the Cardinal's biography.[5]

Gene Hamilton showed little if any of this twist in the personality which so often is the cross of the spiritually minded. In response to the question "Does the student possess a maturity proportional to his age?", Gene writes with a certain candor:

> The level of maturity I possess may be greater than my age. Such a high level allows me to interact with men (specifically in my class) who are older than I am. Yet my age still allows me to develop friendships with those who may be younger than I am.
>
> This interesting characteristic has been both challenging and enjoyable. As a result I have been

able to expand my experiences proportionate to
the age ranges in the House. My sense of convictions is known to those I relate to. My sense of
humor is rather subtle. My ability to relate to everyone is something I treasure.[6]

One of the important tasks of a seminary is to teach a student a balance between the community of fellow seminarians
and the requirements of the apostolate. This must go on while
studies are in progress — no small task. Wisely, the question
of balance is put directly to students of Neumann in their self-
evaluation. Gene's answer is revealing:

Such a balance has been a grace-filled opportunity for me. Being an integral part of the House
is a source of strength and a vehicle for mutual
encouragement. My time outside of the House has
been blessed with being a witness to others, hopefully leading them to a closer union with God and
a better understanding of the many and varied ways
that He calls each of us.[7]

The Neumann self-evaluation contained a question that
could have been devastating for Gene: an inquiry on whether
the student maintained sound physical health. What could he
answer? For years his life had been filled with pain. After he
had been at Neumann just a few weeks, he was so ill that he
received the Sacrament of the Anointing of the Sick and was
home for some time recovering. Luke Sweeney, a close friend,
recalls that he was desperately ill and even hallucinating with
a high fever at that time. Gene's response to the question of
health in this 1994 questionnaire is an answer that would epito-
mize his life for the rest of the time that was left. Knowing
what was to happen, this response will be deeply moving to
almost every reader:

This is the area [physical health] in which my sense of humor has been developed the most. In spite of a number of unfortunate occurrences, I have not let ill health preoccupy my life, while constantly realizing that my health is important.

Reflection upon human suffering is important in the ministry and life of the priest. Such reflection has its proper place. For myself, such reflection is also very personal.

Yet these instances of illness have provided me with opportunities to persevere, while presenting me with the realization that reliance upon God is the cornerstone to growth and health in any area of life.[8]

Around the same time that he wrote this self-evaluation, the mother of his fellow student and close friend Frank Bassett experienced a recurrence of cancer which would, in fact, prove to be terminal. Frank was perplexed about whether to go on to the Spiritual Year at Northampton or perhaps to interrupt his studies in case his mother needed his help. He recalled later that Gene had encouraged him to try to stay in studies unless his mother really needed him and never to forget that he had a vocation to the priesthood. Gene and Mrs. Bassett had a personal conversation during the Easter break, and then his mother agreed that Frank should go on with his studies. Later, the friendship between Gene and Mrs. Bassett would come to a deep level as they both faced terminal cancer at the same time.[9]

The final question of the Neumann self-evaluation, "Who am I?", is what a psychologist would call an "ink blot." Most people would just as soon avoid such a question. In reading these lines it is most important to see a person whom many saw as humble, who no one has said was proud or arrogant, and yet who was not afflicted with the very common pathology of sincere people, self-hate:

I look at myself first and foremost as a servant of God who is called to be with Him and His people. I then stand as an individual called to be relational with others.

My talents and gifts help my individuality become present to those around me. It is my analytical, controlled self that people first see. It is my compassionate, understanding self that people get to know. I am an integrated individual, whose greatest challenge is to make sure that my mind and heart are always working together. I use the talents God has given me, ever mindful that they originated in Him and are to be used for Him.

Most importantly, I am someone who loves. I am a person who knows the beauties and pains associated with loving others. I am someone who is amazed with myself at my ability to love others even more in the most trying of situations. I am someone who realizes this stems from my intense love of God, Who loves me in return, in ways that my mind cannot comprehend, but in ways my heart can experience.[10]

Someone in the course of preparing for this book asked the question perceptively, "Did Gene ever have fun? Was he always on duty?" The question suggested that the person asking this probably had little experience of the spiritual life. A spiritual person, even a dedicated beginner, will have a constant impression of being "on duty." The spiritual life never stops, never takes a vacation. It is a response to the words of Christ, "You shall love the Lord your God with all your heart and with all your soul, and with all your mind, and with all your strength" (Mark 12:30). But this total dedication to the pursuit of God does not preclude recreation and relaxation. St. Francis loved to speak to animals, and St. John of the Cross spent long moments enjoying the startlingly beautiful scenery of Spain, while St. Teresa of Ávila was known as a very good cook. Recall the photos of St. Thérèse of Lisieux made up for the leading role in the nuns' play "Joan of Arc." And Gene's model, Cardinal Cooke, loved baseball and also the great Irish art of conversation.

The following lines written by Luke Sweeney, Gene's seminarian friend, give a picture of someone who loved to be with his friends. The events recalled occurred just a few months before the beginning of the spirituality program at Northampton:

> I can only remember getting together once in the summer with Gene. On the evening of Thursday, June 22, 1995, Gene and I met in Frank's [Bassett's] new room at Dunwoodie. We prayed Vespers and then went to Annunciation Parish in Crestwood to visit with the seminarian Mike Martine, who was there for his summer parish assignment. Mike gave us a tour of the church and rectory and then we went off to eat. We ate in Bronxville or Crestwood at Rockwells, which is near the train tracks. Then we saw a movie. I do not know if it was that night or some other time during the year that Gene told me the story of how Bishop Ahern's zucchetto was eaten by his pastor's dog.[11]

Frank Bassett recalls another incident which happened later when they were at Northampton. During a couple of free hours they went to an arts and crafts fair. There was a booth where someone was doing face painting. Gene thought he should get his face painted and go back to the seminary that way. They laughed and decided that discretion was the better part of valor.[12]

The summer of 1995 was a joyous and busy one for Gene. The obstacles from ill health finally had been overcome. He was preparing for what he anticipated would be a wonderful year of spirituality and faith with people he knew and loved or whom, in the case of the seminarians of the Philadelphia archdiocesan seminary, he was anxious to get to know. He left Neumann to work that summer and to prepare. Monsignor Sullivan, speaking of the seminary in the traditional term "house," sums up not only Gene's year at Neumann but also what its impact would eventually be:

> In the house, Eugene was respected and admired for his intellectual skills, leadership abilities, and fraternal spirit. He was an asset to the house and he and we together took full advantage of his talents and charisms. Eugene looked forward with a kind of spiritual impatience to the spiritual year and his entrance into the major seminary. That year and entrance were to take on their own divine and human qualities that none of us who were his formators could have either desired or willed in human terms. Eugene's spiritual year bore the imprint of the Cross in a way that would sanctify him and many of us.[13]

Mary Immaculate Seminary — A Place to Meet God

The spirituality year, a carefully thought-out program aimed at strengthening the commitment of diocesan seminarians in the Philadelphia archdiocese, had been established for pre-theology students in 1991. This program had many similarities to the novitiate that candidates for religious life are required to make before taking vows. Cardinal O'Connor and Cardinal Anthony Bevilacqua, archbishop of Philadelphia, decided to join forces, and students from the New York archdiocese entered the program in 1994. A school year of spiritual exercises, classes, and workshops on subjects related to the spiritual life was joined to an intense community experience and carefully selected apostolic work focused on the needy and infirm. At the time that Eugene went to Northampton, Father Peter Welsh and Father John Savinski of Philadelphia, who together had initiated the program, were joined by Father Brian Barrett, who represented New York on the staff. From personal experience I can say that this was an outstanding team of men with a new and innovative job.

Mary Immaculate Seminary is a very beautiful building. Arguably the most handsome seminary building in the United States, it is situated high on a hill overlooking the Lehigh Valley and much of northeastern Pennsylvania. It was built as a Vincentian seminary and in recent years has been used by the Spiritual Formation Program while still in the care of the Vincentian Congregation. The chapel, with all its beauty, manages to avoid distracting the visitor, who is almost instantly moved to prayer by simply entering it. Gene, after his long wait at Manhattan and Neumann, was delighted finally to become a theological student, and he plunged into the atmosphere of this beautiful seminary with its engaging program. But in the mysterious ways of Providence this intense happiness was to be very short-lived. In a way, his three weeks at Mary Immaculate were Gene's Palm Sunday.

While at Mary Immaculate Seminary, Gene was in the spiritual care of Father Brian Barrett, an outstanding young priest. In a revealing interview with me immediately after Christmas in 1996, Gene would recall Father Barrett's care for him during his short stay at the seminary and in the long months afterwards in the hospital and at home:

> He was the one who was in charge of my formation while I was at Northampton and also when I was home receiving treatment at Good Samaritan Hospital in Suffern and at Memorial Sloan

Kettering Cancer Center in New York City. Father Barrett was always there and always present and I think in a way he highlighted the importance of the ministry of presence on the part of a priest and how a priest in being present is not just a sign but also becomes an instrument of grace and instrument of God's love to His people.[14]

Father Brian Barrett, who had fought a long and secret battle with thyroid illness, quietly died in his sleep on July 13, 1996. While all involved felt a tremendous sense of loss and prayerful sympathy for Father Barrett's parents and family, this sudden calling-home of an outstanding priest and spiritual support deeply affected Eugene. At Father Barrett's wake at St. Joseph's Seminary Chapel, I noticed Gene wearing a clerical collar, since he had just been given the rank of candidacy to the priesthood ahead of schedule because of his illness. I recall looking at this young man with the deep, thoughtful eyes contrasting so obviously with his friendly smile. I asked myself what his thoughts must be, thanking God at the same time for the faith that we all shared in Christ's resurrection and promise of eternal life.

The three weeks at Northampton would be among the most significant of Gene's life. They were weeks when he was able to enter fully into the program of studies and spiritual formation. He shared the sense of joy and enthusiasm of looking forward to ordination and a life of service in the place of Christ that makes entrance into this demanding vocation possible. For three short weeks he was simply a seminarian; he was about to become a very sick seminarian and then a dying seminarian. These weeks were joyous and engaging, as one might expect, when suddenly, while Gene was working in the sacristy on Saturday, September 16, the onset of a 106-degree fever changed everything.

Endnotes

1. Letter of Monsignor James Sullivan to author, April 21, 1997, 1.
2. Ibid.
3. Self-Evaluation, 2.
4. Ibid., 3, 4.
5. Father B. J. Groeschel, C.F.R. and Terence Weber, *Thy Will Be Done* (New York: Alba House, 1990).
6. Self-Evaluation, 7.
7. Ibid., 9.
8. Ibid., 10.
9. Letter of Frank Bassett, May 30, 1997, 2.
10. Self-Evaluation, 11.
11. Account of Luke Sweeney, 6-7.
12. Letter of Frank Bassett, May 30, 1997, 4.
13. Letter of Monsignor James Sullivan to author, April 21, 1997, 1.
14. December 27, 1996 Interview, 3.

4

A Seminarian Reflects. . .

. . . On Living and Dying With Cancer

Gene

As already mentioned, Gene left an outline and ten preliminary single-spaced pages of an autobiography in his computer. I was only vaguely aware of these pages when I proposed this book. On reading them I realized that much of my work was already done and that the substantive parts of this biography must be quotations from Gene's own work. To do justice to the subject, this must be a book within a book. Considerations of style must not deprive the reader of the thoughtful and poignant words of this young man who was literally pouring out his own soul in an effort to be helpful to his fellow seminarians. We will use Gene's notes selectively, leaving out nothing significant and attempting to follow as closely as possible a chronological order. At times we will clarify and highlight the significance of the narration and relate it to other things that we know about the life of our subject.

Eugene's title was *Servant, Victim, Brother, Listener, Friend*; these are descriptions of the role of a priest given in a homily by Terence Cardinal Cooke at the Chrism Mass of Holy Week in 1977. The Mass at which the Holy Oils are blessed for the year has also become an annual celebration of the priesthood and the day for the clergy to renew their commitments made on the day of ordination, namely, the promises of celibacy and obedience to the bishop. As Gene notes, the Cardinal was preaching as a priest who himself had been struggling with cancer secretly for over a decade at this time.

Eugene outlines his purposes in writing this book in the fairly complete introduction:

> What follows here are a series of reflections on my journey as a seminarian living and dying with cancer. A seminarian is one studying for the priesthood, forming himself and being formed, to one day be ordained to the service of God, His Church, and His People as a Priest of Jesus Christ. While not a priest myself, I have had ample opportunity in the midst of this unique experience to reflect upon the qualities of a priest outlined in Cardinal Cooke's Chrism Mass homily. It summarized his understanding of the priesthood; it became a blueprint for my own vocation, and thus the title for these reflections.
>
> . . . The titles/chapter headings for these reflections highlight some of the issues that were close to my heart and very much a part of my interior being. I am a private person by nature; this book

puts into words what I may not have expressed
verbally in life. It is my original intention that these
reflections become public after my death. If you
are reading this, that is probably true. It is important that everyone knows that the reflections are
my own, therefore any inconsistencies, errors,
omissions, misstatements, or misinformation are
the fault of myself alone. For these, I apologize to
anyone who may have been offended. My intention was never to hurt anyone or make them feel
as if they were not a part of this story.

These reflections . . . are targeted for a specific
audience, namely seminarians, those studying for
the priesthood. If they are of benefit to seminarians or anyone else for that matter, that is God's
work, not mine.[1]

It is moving to note the dedication Gene wrote for his unfinished book. It is significant that Joseph Cardinal Bernardin,
Archbishop of Chicago, had died on November 14, 1996. His
death had made a deep impression on many, as had Cardinal
Cooke's, because they both did battle with cancer while con-
tinuing a full round of duties as shepherds of huge dioceses.
Because of the reference to Cardinal Bernardin, we can date
this outline as having been written after November 14, 1996:

Dedication

To the Servant of God Terence Cardinal
Cooke, Archbishop of New York, and Joseph
Cardinal Bernardin, Archbishop of Chicago. Two
priests who, by the Will of the Father, were con-
figured to the Crucified Christ, Priest and Vic-
tim, through cancer; AND Stephen Robert
Sowinski, a seventeen-year-old studying to be a
Catholic priest at Cathedral Preparatory Semi-

nary, Elmhurst, New York, who died of leukemia after an unsuccessful bone marrow transplant; and, Joseph Grampp, a young boy at Memorial Sloan Kettering Cancer Center who himself thought of priesthood before he died.[2]

As we will see further on, this dedication indicates that Eugene in many ways had identified with his fellow patients during his hospitalizations. We will see that sometimes he made the Stations of the Cross going from room to room, visiting each seriously ill patient, and recalling one of the events in the last day of the life of Christ. Certainly this is a somewhat unusual reversal of what most dying people experience. Because of the anxiety produced by possibility of death, many people must struggle with a kind of self-centered regression and narrowing of their awareness to their own needs. This is totally understandable. At least at the time that Gene was writing this book the opposite process was in motion; he was reaching out to others in the same painful situation.

Eugene also indicates that he was going to ask Bishop Edwin F. O'Brien, at that time rector of St. Joseph's Seminary, to write the preface. It would be this bishop (who at this writing has been appointed Coadjutor Archbishop of the Military Ordinariate) who would confer Holy Orders on Eugene in the most unusual circumstances, literally at the hour of death.

Trusting in God

Eugene's outline of his autobiography begins with a chapter entitled "Trusting in God." It is very well-thought-out and gives all of the facts. Thus we can continue our narrative with Gene's own account of the events and his profound reaction to them. These passages are beautifully revealing and remove the obligation of most biographers to try to interpret the reactions of the subject to important events in his own life:

A Seminarian Reflects...

On Sunday, September 17, 1995 (my brother Tom's birthday), I came home from the Spirituality Year Program at Northampton. . . . Exhibiting a high fever, difficulty breathing, rapid pulse rate, and a rising blood pressure, I saw my pediatrician the next day. That Monday I completed a chest X ray, chest CAT scan, and consultation with a thoracic surgeon by 6:00 p.m. that evening. Examining the CAT scan in the doctor's office, I found myself staring at a large mass in the center of the chest cavity, a tumor placing pressure on my lungs and pushing against my heart. I knew that I was looking at something foreign in my body, something that didn't belong, something that was aggressively taking any available room in a very confined space. I knew I was looking at cancer.

My mother asked that surgeon what would happen after he biopsied the mass. He turned to her and said we would have to see an oncologist. As we drove home that night, I remember telling my mother that, "This is what trusting in God is all about." It was perhaps a reflex statement on my part, because I really didn't think about it before saying it, yet it came from somewhere within my being. I was leaning back on my faith, a faith that had sustained me throughout the years of school, growing up, tragedies and celebrations, fears and joys. I would slowly come to realize over time just what that statement meant.[3]

The human mind deals with life by seeking to adjust to it with the resources available. When the necessary means of adjustment are not available or are not properly used, a person regresses and either sinks into deep depression or desperately denies reality and makes useless attempts to pretend it is not there. Physicians and others assisting the terminally ill have come to respect denial as a defense mechanism and they are understandably not anxious to disturb it. Unfortunately, this attitude often deprives the patient with strong faith of an opportunity to practice the theological virtue of hope and to look forward productively to preparing for his meeting with God (called in Scripture the judgment) and to entering into eternal life.

None of us knows what we will do or not do when we have to face the reality of impending death with its earthly finality. Some crumble, some deny, some bravely go on, and some by faith in God prepare for a new reality which is believed to surpass all that this very short and fragile life can offer. Obviously religious people should do best with the knowledge of their own impending death and, in fact, they often do "cope with it" quite well. Those with little or no faith who have not yet really faced their own mortality may try to reduce dying by a complex system of denials. Few people, other than the real believers, ever look death in the eye as it is coming toward them. A number of genuinely religious people, and especially devout Christians, use their resources and walk toward this universal human experience of death with the attitude expressed by St. Paul, "O death, where is thy victory? O death, where is thy sting?" (1 Corinthians 15:55). This is precisely what Eugene Hamilton does in his unfinished book. Creatively he looks for touching analogies between his catastrophic physical symptoms and a number of profound symbols of his faith:

> The placement of the tumor in the mediastinal area of the chest cavity and the pressure it was putting on the heart and lungs forged a direct connection with my interior life. As my breathing became labored, I turned to the Holy Spirit, the Breath of Life. Each gasp for air was both a plea, a prayer, a hope, and a fight. I not only wanted and needed

air, but I wanted and needed God. Each breath was both my first and my last. Each breath was truly a Breath of Life.

In examining that initial CAT scan, I noticed that the heart had been displaced by the tumor. For someone who was always checking his motives and trying to determine whether his heart was in the right place, this was a most ironic situation. My physical heart was out of place; was my spiritual heart also? Clearly the concept of trusting in God became all the more real. The task before the doctors was to somehow shrink or remove this mass thus returning the physical heart to its natural place. Would the Divine Physician do the same for my spiritual heart?[4]

The Process of Preparation for Death

Anyone who has even a moderate knowledge of the processes of spiritual development and has had the opportunity to assist a person with terminal illness knows that those who accept God's call from this world, even with some difficulty, make years of progress in a short time. People can grow twenty years in twenty days when death has focused their attention on what is really important and they have accepted God's will that they soon depart from this life.

This process of rapid spiritual growth is remarkably illustrated in the notes that Gene kept in his computer. At a time of great stress the familiar symbols of faith and devotion will take on new importance and become intensely meaningful. A dying person with faith will derive strength from reciting the Rosary, or praying before a particular picture, or reading passages from the Psalms or New Testament. The importance of symbols and devotions is amply illustrated in Gene's autobiography. His great fortitude in having these signs of faith available sadly highlights the harm that has been done to those who have been deprived of these grace-filled signs during life and at the hour of death:

> Visible to the eye of my mind at this time was the classic picture of the Sacred Heart of Jesus. Our Lord not only shows us His Heart, but He exposes its wounds, its radiance, its drops of Blood. Our Lord doesn't just expose His Heart, but He points us towards it and the flame of Love that rises from it. Was He now pointing at my heart through the hand of the surgeon? How does one respond when our Lord points His finger at us? I was left completely open before Him, unsure as to whether I should look at myself or tremble in His sight given the uncertainty and mystery associated with the point of that Finger. This was no Uncle Sam pointing and saying, "I want you!" This was Jesus pointing and saying nothing, stretching out His Hand and remaining silent.[5]

Anyone who has gained the insights into Eugene Hamilton's inner life discussed up to now realizes that this was no superficial young man. We already see in him signs of a wisdom beyond his years. But without implying any previous superficiality at all, we must now see him moving into the deep waters of human existence which are there for us all but which are regretfully so seldom explored.

To understand what Gene experienced from the time of his initial diagnosis till death, we must consider his life in the light of the traditional teaching of the ways of the spiritual life or journey. His own writings clearly indicate that he was completing two essential phases of the spiritual life, mature faith and complete trust. These two steps follow on a complete inner conversion or moral integration (that is, the establishment of a life of consistent moral integrity). While all seriously involved in the spiritual life live moral lives, believe in God and trust in Him, those completing these phases of the spiritual journey bring these two virtues to the highest level of personal integration. Because trust in God is the theological virtue of hope, those completing the first, or purgative, way will have achieved a high level of faith and hope preparing them for charity.

Christian faith must not be understood as simply an intellectual conviction. People become deeply convinced, even to the point of sacrificing their lives to ideologies that are far different from any gift of faith. Some have gladly died for political ideologies, even evil ones like Nazism and Communism, in our own times. Oddly enough, they may have done this out of a twisted or confused sense of altruism. But Christian faith goes beyond intellectual conviction. It is a personal relationship with Our Savior, not only as He is known historically, but as He is present by grace to the individual believer. A person without an experience of mature faith will find this idea of the actual presence of Christ inconceivable or even laughable — it is only a "pie in the sky." The same can be said of Christian hope. Hope is not simply optimism, which can at best be a form of courage. The Christian virtue of hope is focused on eternal salvation and extends to all other needs and desires only when these serve the goal of eternal salvation and ultimate sanctification.

I doubt that Gene was at all aware when he typed his autobiography into his computer after receiving his terminal diagnosis that he was describing in a most accurate way the second and third steps of the purgative way of the spiritual journey, the steps of faith and hope.[6]

Because of the reality of the situation, and because he was already and apparently had been a very highly integrated, morally committed Christian, and because he had worked hard since high school in having a faith-filled life, he describes his struggle with cancer more in terms of hope or trust — although this virtue already requires a firm faith. He often referred to trust in God as faith — but it really is a faith and hope leading to absolute trust that he is writing about. It is not unusual for us to use words like "faith" or "trust" interchangeably, although they have slightly different meanings. We need to bear this in mind as we read the following quotations which, properly understood, are a succinct description of the completion of the purgative or first of the three ways of the spiritual journey:

Once again, I was saved by faith. "Jesus, I Trust in You" became my response. It became the words that I clung to, even as I sent them to God. These are the words that form the core of the message of Divine Mercy, as outlined in a series of revelations given to Blessed Maria Faustina in visions and locutions by Jesus Christ. The Divine Mercy devotion was one that had brought me considerable consolation over the years. A seminarian in the midst of formation must critically examine himself, his actions, motives, intentions, his very heart. He must face his own sinfulness, unworthiness, and nakedness before almighty God. Pleading for the infinite Divine Mercy was not just a way to avoid God's disappointment but rather to focus upon His infinite goodness. This initially led me to feel even smaller in the sight of God; yet a growing confidence in Him also became evident. Perhaps the greatest test to my devotion to the Divine Mercy came in the present situation of cancer. Now, each and every day, I would have to practice trust in God, always mindful of my own sinfulness and need of forgiveness. When faced with a life threatening illness, this aspect of my relationship with God took on a particular urgency that was renewed each day. The result of this was a growing realization of the gift of life that God had given to me for the particular day. The challenge was living that gift as He wanted.[7]

Abandonment and Peace

Many readers may be unfamiliar with the expression "abandonment to God" (or "abandonment to Divine Providence"). Some may find the phrase annoyingly traditional and perhaps even reminiscent of what they consider misguided religious attitudes. This term "abandonment" was proposed especially by a number of French spiritual writers in the seventeenth and eighteenth centuries. The concept of the total entrusting of all one's life and experience to God was advocated by St. Claude de la Colombière, the spiritual director of the mystic visionary of the Sacred Heart of Jesus, St. Margaret Mary Alacoque. It became very much part of the devotion to the Sacred Heart. Perhaps this term received its highest level of understanding a century later in the book which was to have the very name, *Abandonment to Divine Providence*, as its title.[8] This was a series of profound conferences written by Pere Jean Pierre de Caussade, S.J., to cloistered nuns (in fact, I gave a copy of this book to Eugene in October of 1996, but by that time he was already well rooted in this personal expression of faith and trust).

Actually the idea of abandonment to God is biblical — the roots of abandonment can be found in the trust in God spoken of by the Jewish scriptures and especially in the absolute "Fiat" of Mary and the total acceptance of the Messiah Himself in the Agony in the Garden and on the Cross. The words "Thy will be done" have been the bedrock of all great Christian spirituality, including that of Augustine, the Eastern Fathers, Francis, Teresa of Àvila, John of the Cross, and on to Thérèse of Lisieux and the saints of the twentieth century. This step of placing all of one's life and cares at the disposal of the divine will even finds a strong echo in the third step of the spiritual program of

Alcoholics Anonymous. This step, calling for a decision to turn all in life over to the care of God, puts into modern terms what the saints have always known. Gene, with a certain and clear intuition, found his peace in this concept of acceptance as the highest expression of faith and hope — but not without a struggle:

> The concepts of abandonment and surrender also came into play. There also began an immediate tension. The initial reaction of a patient, myself included, is to reach for any type of control over one's life that you can get. A rather reserved and hesitant person by nature, I now had to put my life not only in God's Hands, but the hands of physicians, nurses, technicians, and others as well. I was also no longer able to trust even myself — my own body had deceived me and had begun manufacturing cells that were meant to destroy the very life-giving cells that formed my physical being.
>
> To be quite honest, I was forced to surrender — to my body, my doctors, and my God. Over time, I abandoned myself — to my condition, my doctors, and my God. Needless to say, this was done at considerable personal price. I can only say with certainty that I completely abandoned myself to God. The other parties were grudgingly "surrendered to." Yet, it was that abandonment to God that made such surrenders easier. Let me be clear, this was an ongoing struggle. While accepting the overall situation and each individual instance associated with the disease, there was a desire to take control and fight by myself. This was a natural response, but I also had to take into account God and His Will in addition to those who could help me here on earth. I was faced with wanting to do

things myself and handing my life over to others or the Other. Perhaps this is one of the essential struggles associated with a vocation, any vocation.[9]

Gene emphasizes that this philosophy of abandonment would guide his life through the fears, the tragic disappointments, and the growing spiritual hopes that the coming months would bring.

Endnotes

1. *Servant, Victim, Brother, Listener, Friend*, 3. This manuscript thereafter referred to as *Servant*.
2. Ibid., 1.
3. Ibid., 4.
4. Ibid.
5. Ibid., 4-5.
6. For a discussion of these stages, confer my book, *Spiritual Passages* (New York: Crossroad, 1995).
7. *Servant*, 5.
8. Father Jean Pierre de Caussade, S.J, *Abandonment to Divine Providence* (New York: Doubleday, 1995).
9. *Servant*, 5.

5

Months of Treatment — Days of Learning

The Hamilton Family

From mid-September 1995, to June 20, 1996, Gene and his family lived through the all-too-familiar roller-coaster rides of glimmers of hope and deep disappointment which are the familiar experience of those with cancer. We have already examined many of the spiritual steps that he took in those nine months and the ever-deepening life of prayer that was going on with him — a prayer that reflected an ever-growing union with God. The external events of those months are, in fact, of less importance than the inner spiritual events whose effects would be everlasting; however, these external events are important for us to fully appreciate what was about to happen.

Fortunately, Gene's mother, Margaret, kept an informal diary of her own thoughts. Anyone who has lived through the terrible ups and downs of pre-terminal cancer with a loved one will recognize all too poignantly the emotions, desperate prayers, and instinctive terrors that reach beyond the assurances of faith because they are not intellectual. What threatens the life of someone dear to us evokes responses that are instinctual and beyond the control of the mind. Many see themselves in the image of Our Lady of Sorrows and the words applied to her, "Is it nothing to you, all you who pass by? Look and see if there is any sorrow like my sorrow" (Lamentations 1:12). Even the prayers of the Messiah in the garden should warn us that the human mind is not always in complete control of the body's reactions to its impending destruction.

We are grateful to Margaret Hamilton for sharing her thoughts. The entry for September 27, 1995, says it all to those who know the experience of seeing a loved one approach death:

> Well, Lord, today is your day. We're here, Gene and I, waiting for the start of the chemotherapy in Good Samaritan Hospital, Suffern. He is so brave, so confident that Your Will *will* be done. I think back to nine days ago. It seems forever, so long ago. I remember looking at the CAT scan in the surgeon's office and silently praying, "Oh, God! Jesus, please help us, Cardinal Cooke, pray for us."

No one used the word cancer. Instead, we were told that Gene would have to see an oncologist. We waited in the parking lot for his father. "Mary, our mother, help me stay calm for my son's sake, please," I prayed.

The tests and biopsy confirmed the suspicions of the specialists — cancer. Gene is upbeat. "I shall not die, but live." Father Brian Barrett calls and comes that first of many Saturdays that he would visit. He shares with all of us his own battle five years before with thyroid cancer. He gives us strength and hope. Here is the nurse. The chemo is ready. Gene is ready. I can't help but think of Jesus tied to the pillar with ropes.[1]

The next three months were times of trial but hope. Gene learned the role of being a disciple-patient. Despite the storm of anxiety, the strong voice of faith and the prayerful tools of Christian devotion, now so sadly lost to so many, were all there to guide and sustain him:

Monday, September eighteenth began with a visit to my doctor, a subsequent X ray and CAT scan, and a visit to a surgeon that night. What I saw on the films that night was a massive tumor pressing against the heart and lungs, accounting for my inability to breathe. Given the circumstances, I found myself praying to the Holy Spirit that night, reflecting upon how He is the Breath of Life. I thought about the wind blowing and the Apostles in the Upper Room beginning their new lives of ministry, and wondered whether I was about to lose my own life. I prayed the words of Cardinal Mercier, "O, Holy Spirit, beloved of my soul . . . Enlighten me, guide me, strengthen me, console me. . . ." And so, with the help of the Holy Spirit, my trust in God deepened and grew.

The Wednesday of that same week, surgery was performed to remove a part of the tumor to see whether it was cancerous. Given its proximity to the heart, I was reminded of the Sacred Heart of Jesus, realizing how closely that Heart is connected to the Eucharist, and how wounded that Heart was. And so, as I slipped into unconsciousness, I prayed, "Sacred Heart of Jesus, I place my trust in you."[2]

Margaret describes Gene's struggle as she saw it. These two descriptions, one autobiographical and the other from his mother, powerfully present the beginning of what was to be for Gene the definitive struggle of his life, one which would bring Gene spiritually much further than most of us expect to get in a lifetime:

From September 1995 through the beginning of December 1995, the treatments went as scheduled — five days in the hospital; then home for two weeks with a weekly chemo treatment those weeks. Gene never complained. The only thing he ever said was, "I'm tired." When some of the medication affected his vision I had the honor of reading to him. We said Morning Prayer and the Rosary every morning when he was home. In the hospital, we said the Rosary. Gene tried to keep to a filled schedule of formal prayer and spiritual reading. He was blessed by having "the Chapel Channel" on [TV] when he was in Good Samaritan. He was able to watch the daily Mass and weekly televised Rosary. He often said that his bed was the back seat of the chapel.[3]

For Gene the trial was to be out of the seminary. He had waited for years and now he could not be there. He did receive and appreciate much encouragement from faculty and students:

> It was during this time that I received a great deal of encouragement from Rev. Brian Barrett and Rev. Richard O'Gorman. Father Barrett related to me his own struggle with this illness and gave me a renewed sense of hope. Father O'Gorman assured me of his prayers during this difficult time. John Cardinal O'Connor telephoned and made me realize the importance of the suffering I would undergo. The then-Monsignor Edwin O'Brien encouraged me and always made me feel a part of the seminary community at a time when I was physically isolated from that community. I was not alone.
>
> My thoughts turned to Terence Cardinal Cooke, a man I met only once, at my father's ordination, a man about whom I had done a presentation in a college religion class highlighting his sanctity, a priest who himself had cancer. His motto, *Fiat Voluntas Tua* — "Thy Will be Done," came to mind as I listened to the doctor. I realized that, at least initially, I would not be returning to Northampton and that the bond between my classmates on the Spiritual Year and me would be a spiritual one. The chemotherapy began one week later. By that time, I had already united my sufferings with those of Jesus with the hope that they would take on salvific meaning.[4]

The Visit of the Pope

A great disappointment for Gene was to miss the visit of Pope John Paul II to New York and to his own seminary. For a

seminarian outside of Rome to be at home for a papal visit is a
one-in-a-million experience. Gene could not be there, but the
disappointment taught him much about being a disciple. He
learned what it meant to have Christ with you at all times:

> Although terribly disappointed not to be able
> to be at Dunwoodie for the Pope's visit due to a
> low white-cell count, Gene united with the semi-
> narians in spirit and prayer. Tears welled up in his
> eyes and ours when he was mentioned by name
> during Evening Prayer.[5]

Gene recalls the visit of the Pope in his spiritual evaluation
of the year:

> The visit of Pope John Paul II to America, and
> especially to New York, was another significant
> spiritual experience. While not physically present
> at any of the events in which seminarians partici-
> pated, I felt united in prayer with my brothers in
> Christ in the Chapel of SS. Peter and Paul. Being
> mentioned in the intercessions overwhelmed me
> with a sense of gratitude and reminded me that we
> are never alone in our trials and sufferings.[6]

Gene did not waste any time or energy on self-pity. As you
read of his spiritual experiences, recall that at this time he was
faced with the awesome possibility of death:

> October was also Respect Life Month. When I
> first learned I had cancer, I offered up my suffer-
> ings for those whose lives were threatened in any
> way. During October, I used Cardinal Cooke's Pas-
> toral Letter as a basis for reflection on the "gift of
> life." During this time I was coming to a greater

realization that this life was not my own and that His kingdom and His will were what we sought after and hoped for.[7]

In the meantime Gene's parents and loved ones had to live with their feelings. Gene's absence from the Mass of Pope John Paul II in Central Park planted an idea that came to fruition only fifteen months later at the crucial moment of his ordination. Margaret continues:

During this time a fierce spiritual battle was going on in my own soul. I scarcely dared to ask then-Monsignor O'Brien personally to ask the Pope to pray for Gene. Gene was so confident and trusting in God, and I was terrified of both the diagnosis and of the future. I sincerely believed that God wanted Gene to be His priest. I kept re-calling the story of the woman in the Gospels — if only I could touch Him, He will heal my son. I must see the Pope, but how can that happen! Gene needs me at home. Three days before the Mass in Central Park, it was determined that Tom (Gene's brother) needed someone to be with him. He was one of the youth selected to receive Holy Com-munion from our Holy Father. A friend came to stay with Gene.

Before Mass, Father Benedict came over to me and said that he was praying for Gene Sr. and me. I felt the shell of bravery crack. I felt as though Gene Sr. and I were being carried to the throne of the Father. When I saw Pope John Paul shortly af-terwards all I could say was, "Jesus, please heal my son. O Lord, I am not worthy but only say the word and my son will be healed." I felt at peace, confident that all of us were in the hand of God. I really began to trust and believe that God's hand was in this.[8]

God Does Not Cause Evil

Gene in the meantime had to deal with the very real possibility of his own death. Most people refuse to think about this most important journey. In his Spiritual Year Evaluation for November he writes:

> The communion of saints and the souls in purgatory were the basis of my reflections as the chemotherapy progressed. I thought of St. Joseph, who held the Christ Child in his hands, and the connection with the priest who holds the living Christ in his hands as well. I thought of St. Peregrine, the patron of cancer patients, and St. John Neumann. I offered up my sufferings for the souls in Purgatory and reflected on the meaning of human suffering.
>
> This was also when I began, along with my classmates at Northampton, the preparation for total consecration to Jesus through Mary as outlined by St. Louis de Montfort. This continued until December eighth, the Feast of the Immaculate Conception.
>
> I learned a very important lesson during this time as well, namely the importance of letting others help me. It required an admission by me that I couldn't do everything on my own and made me realize that letting others help me might actually help them. It was a further admission that I was helpless, a concept that I struggled with and ultimately left in the hands of God.[9]

Margaret, Gene Sr., and Tom were now being powerfully drawn into a mystery that is beyond us all — the mystery of death and life beyond it. They had been there, of course, from the very beginning, but now they would know more and more clearly each day that the hand of the Lord was on their son and brother. We often enough think that prayer is a means to change the mind of God. It is really meant to help us use God's grace to bring good out of evil. St. Augustine in his *Soliloquies* says that God does not cause evil, but He keeps evil from becoming worse, and He even reveals to those who flee to Him that ultimately evil is not real at all, because He is the Father of life and the Father of all good and in Him we shall find all good.[10]

Gene found himself grappling with the possibility of a new treatment. He writes that Father Barrett "helped me realize that God's Will was being carried out."[11]

The road of Gene and the Hamilton family took another painful turn. Margaret writes:

> It was December 27, 1995, our twenty-fifth wedding anniversary, and here we were sitting in Sloan Kettering, New York City. The next two days were filled with anxiety and fear. News that the tumor markers had risen erased any question about whether Gene would undergo this new treatment of stem-cell rescue combined with high-dose chemotherapy. He had to if he was to live. How will we be able to get Gene to these treatments. . . ?
>
> This time it was Father Barrett and Monsignor O'Brien to the rescue. Monsignor O'Brien called St. Catherine of Siena Priory and made arrangements for Gene to stay there during treatments. What graciousness and hospitality they showed! Gene had a room there. There was a peace about Gene. He loved being able to visit the chapel at any time. The support of this Dominican community strengthened him.[12]

The drama of the months of treatment at Memorial Sloan Kettering is important for us to see. St. Thérèse of Lisieux speaks of "the monotony of sacrifice." We have observed that Gene was a real disciple while in the hospital. This generalization takes on concrete dimensions when we read Margaret's account:

> The treatments at Sloan were rough — nine hospitalizations between January 4 and early April. Never did Gene complain. He showed courage, determination, and he kept his dry sense of humor as well. His chemo treatments started on January 5, the feast of St. John Neumann. The prayer "Passion of Christ, sustain me" became Gene's. Gene remained in control of his treatment. He knew what medications were being given and in what dosages. He learned how to give himself injections of neupogen to boost his white cell count. When he gave it to himself twice a day he would refer to his "a.m. leg" and his "p.m. leg."
>
> Gene was loved by the nurses. He joked with them. One nurse would go out to McDonald's on her break at night and get him milk shakes. Several of them kept in contact with Gene after he left Sloan.
>
> When Gene could he received Communion daily. He loved to pray for the people whose names Father Gannon gave him. He felt very close to a fifteen-year-old boy named Joseph Grampp. When Joseph died, Gene was very sorrowful.
>
> Visits from Bishop O'Brien delighted him. He was so happy when the Bishop called him personally to tell him that he would be ordained a bishop in March. Bishop O'Brien made him feel a part of the seminary family. Gene always felt comfortable in his presence. Not only did he respect Bishop O'Brien, he loved him.

Father Barrett was another important support. He reinforced the spiritual bond between Gene and his classmates at Northampton. Father Barrett was always there for Gene and for our family.[13]

Gene's reaction to the treatment again reveals the growing depth of his faith. His new treatment, requiring the purification of stem blood-cells, took six hours a day in a procedure that is externally similar to dialysis. He notes that the preparatory surgery was on the feast of St. Elizabeth Ann Seton and the treatments began the next day, the feast of St. John Neumann. Again he found strength in spiritual analogies. Those who might smile at the simplicity of such faith could do well to recall that many hospital patients find solace in soap operas and other useless offerings of the media:

> Harvesting the stem cells from the blood stream involved filtering my blood through a machine (blood pheresis), a procedure which lasted for six hours each day for three days. Lying in a bed next to the machine gave me a unique opportunity to reflect upon the Precious Blood of Christ and I read Father Faber's book, *The Precious Blood*.[14]

Death Comes Close

While Gene was going through these painful treatments, Mrs. Bassett, the mother of his friend Frank, came to the end of her suffering on January 11, 1996. A strong bond had developed between them, and they often talked because they were going through the same trials. Gene was too weak and vulnerable to infection to attend Mrs. Bassett's funeral, but he and his parents went to the funeral parlor when no one else was there. The Hamiltons stayed for two hours, praying and chatting with Frank. He recalls that Gene wanted to know what her death was like. Frank explained that it was very peaceful. It would be just about a year later that Frank would attend a very similar and peaceful death in the Hamiltons' living room. The death of Mrs. Bassett must have been very frightening to the young seminarian so deeply involved with his own fight for life; but Frank recalls, "He was always there for someone else, no matter what it meant for him."[15] Frank would recall later:

> My Mom told me how Gene's courage and faith through his diagnosis really affected her. I saw a change in her, although she was of a strong faith herself. . . . Gene told me after my mother passed away that she really gave him a boost in the way which she was dealing with her cancer.[16]

A Jewish Friend

Margaret recalls a touching incident. Gene's hospital roommate at the time was a Hasidic Jewish man who was in the terminal period. Again, the presence of Cardinal Cooke was felt. The prayer leaflets for the beatification of the Cardinal contained Psalm 119, along with traditional Christian prayers, because so many of the friends of the Cardinal were Jewish and they were interested in the cause. Margaret recalls:

> In one case, his roommate was a Lubavitcher Jewish man. Gene helped him by ignoring his own comfort and turning lights on and off for him on the Sabbath. They became good friends. By the end of Gene's stay, Gene had given him a prayer card of Cardinal Cooke. Together they prayed the psalm on the inside. On subsequent hospital visits, this man's wife visited Gene. She told me how much they loved Gene.[17]

Gene also made new friends with the Dominican Friars at St. Catherine's. Gene recalls gratefully:

> The Dominican friars treated me as one of their own. Always willing to help, they gave me access to the Friars' Chapel where the Blessed Sacrament was reserved. I would be able to continue to be in the Real Presence of Christ and gain the necessary strength to continue. In between the hospital admissions and the twice-weekly outpatient visits, I would stay with the Dominicans and spend my time in the chapel.[18]

Gene was particularly grateful to Father William Gannon, O.P., the chaplain who brought him Holy Communion every day and provided him with a list of patients who needed prayers. Gene sent this list on to Northampton.[19]

The Table of the Cross

After substantial chemotherapy had reduced the tumor, Gene was able to undergo surgery to remove the cancerous mass. Gene went home to try to build up his body and at the same time to observe Holy Week by following the services on TV, since he was too ill to risk infection by going to church. Monsignor Farley offered Mass at the Hamilton home on the previous Sunday; it was the first time Gene had been able to attend Mass for a while. On April 23, the tumor was removed by a "clamshell thoracotomy." Gene's recollection of the surgery is deeply moving:

> Once in the operating room, I was placed on a T-shaped table with my arms secured to the ends of the "T." Since I was still awake, I had some time to realize that there was perhaps no better way to face surgery, death, life, or the priesthood than this. With arms outstretched and placing myself in the hands of others, I said a few words of encouragement to the surgical team, breathed

in my anesthesia, and repeated the words, "Jesus,
I trust in You."[20]

I arrived at the hospital at about nine in the evening not
expecting to see Gene at all, but to encourage his parents. I
just missed them, but the nurse to my surprise suggested that
I speak to Gene. I whispered his name somewhat reluctantly.
I was amazed by the response he made with his eyes closed,
"Good evening, Father Benedict. It was really kind of you to
come." I gave him a blessing and left, wondering what kind
of man this was who could think of someone else in these
circumstances. Margaret recalls that she told Gene to say the
Holy Name of Jesus over and over. The answer was, "I've
been saying it for months."

I Have Seen Christ

During the next two months Gene was at home and much
involved with his parents. It was a time of quiet suffering and
rapid spiritual growth. He enjoyed going to daily Mass and making a daily holy hour, doing his spiritual reading, reciting the
Rosary and the Divine Mercy Chaplet. He worked in the pre-
Cana program and helped prepare a class of Confirmation candidates. Word was getting around that Gene was on the mend.

The smiles and good humor of Gene, however, covered up
a great deal of pain and suffering. Our story does not concern
a naive person, or one who had the defenses to take life lightly.
For Gene this was a time of experiencing the salvific meaning
of suffering. The following remarks, which are actually the
conclusion of his Spiritual Year Self-Evaluation, written on May
15, 1996, reveal perhaps more than anything he wrote up till
the beginning of his book the following December what was
really going on inside of him:

> In a theme that Pope John Paul II has continu-
> ally touched upon, suffering can indeed take on

salvific meaning. Good can overcome evil. Many good things have resulted from this past year. I have been a witness to the tremendous power of prayer. I have continued to grow in my relationship with God. I have seen Christ in the faces of those who were suffering and those who were comforting.

My relationship with my classmates has been primarily a spiritual one. We have been united in prayer, although physically separated by circumstance. My family has supported me throughout this experience. Perhaps the most difficult aspect of this illness was realizing that they were experiencing it also. Yet they were a great support and inspiration, always understanding and there to help. They spent countless hours at my bedside, praying and just being there, giving me the strength that I needed.

Through this experience, many more people have also come to know of the exemplary life of Terence Cooke. Perhaps more people now will turn to him and ask his intercession. For myself, the example of Cardinal Cooke, in his priesthood, his illness, and his letters, has been an inspiration and cause of consolation. At my father's ordination, he put his hand on my chest right above where the tumor would develop. My devotion to him didn't begin with this illness, it only increased. I would often repeat his episcopal motto, *"Fiat Voluntas Tua,"* while I was receiving my chemotherapy. Today, that motto represents a hope for my life, that I can do the Will of God.

Finally, I was the recipient of that grace Cardinal Cooke referred to in his pastoral letter. The gift of life I have received has been given to me by

God and it is indeed a blessing. Now, it is my belief and my hope that God will continue to guide it at every step as I journey on the road to what I believe to be His Will for me, the Priesthood of Jesus Christ.

This past year I have had many opportunities to reflect upon Sacred Scripture. It is this passage which best describes my spiritual experience during the year:

Psalm 116:1-9

I love the Lord for he has heard
the cry of my appeal;
for he turned his ear to me
in the day when I called him.
They surrounded me, the snares of death,
with the anguish of the tomb;
they caught me, sorrow and distress,
I called on the Lord's name.
O Lord my God, deliver me!
How gracious is the Lord, and just;
our God has compassion.
The Lord protects the simple hearts;
I was helpless so he saved me.
Turn back, my soul, to your rest
for the Lord has been good;
he has kept my soul from death,
my eyes from tears
and my feet from stumbling.
I will walk in the presence of the Lord
in the land of the living.[21]

Endnotes

1. Diary of Margaret Hamilton, 1.
2. Spiritual Year Self-Evaluation, May 15, 1996, 4-5.

3. Diary, 2.
4. Evaluation, 5.
5. Diary, 2.
6. Evaluation, 7.
7. Ibid.
8. Diary, 2-4.
9. Evaluation, 7-8.
10. *Soliloquies*, Book 1, Chapter 1, Number 2, quoted in Father B.J. Groeschel, C.F.R., *Augustine: Major Writings* (New York: Crossroad, 1995), 47.
11. Evaluation, 8.
12. Diary, 4-5.
13. Ibid., 5-6.
14. Evaluation, 9.
15. Letter of Frank Bassett, May 30, 1997, 7.
16. Ibid.
17. Diary, 7.
18. Evaluation, 10.
19. Ibid., 11.
20. Ibid., 12-13.
21. Ibid., 13-15.

6

They Caught Me —Sorrow and Distress

Margaret and Gene

Gene and his mother had an appointment on June 20, the feast of St. Aloysius Gonzaga, at Memorial Sloan Kettering Hospital. The surgery and the reports after had been hopeful. Now the words of Psalm 116 were going to become all the more meaningful. May I suggest that you take a deep breath before reading Margaret's description of the meeting with the doctor?

The room facing the East River was cold, despite it being June. Gene and I had prayed the Rosary in the car on the way into the city. "Mary, Mother of Priests, help us. Pray for us," we had prayed. The doctor and nurse walked in, greeted us, popped the CAT scans up on the screen. The doctor explained to Gene that the cancer had returned. He showed him the tumor in the center of the chest, the tumor in the upper left quadrant, and the small protrusions at the base of the right lung. I remember Gene getting up out of his seat and walking over to the screens. He studied the scans as the doctor explained what was going on. I prayed, "Jesus, help him. Please be with us. Mary, Mother of Priests, help him. Mary, Mother of Jesus, help me. Cardinal Cooke, please pray for us." Gene sat down again, and asked the doctor what he planned to do, i.e., what treatment he planned. The doctor told him that there was really little he could do. He discussed a study that was going on at Indiana University, but we were told that there was no proven success rate. The doctor mentioned that it (the cancer) could be treated with etoposide for a while, but that he didn't expect results. Then very quietly, Gene asked, "Am I going to die?" The doctor replied, "Yes. Your condition is terminal." Gene then asked, "How long do I have?" The reply: "A few months."

As Gene's mother, I was shaken to the root of my whole being. I looked at Gene. His eyes, always so expressive, revealed a certain strength and courage, as well as a deep sadness. We left Sloan in silence and went across the street to St. Catherine of Siena Church. I watched from a pew as Gene knelt at the altar rail before the Blessed Sacrament.

He looked so alone, so little. My thoughts flashed back to April 1980, the day of his first Communion, when he had stood alone at the head of the aisle in St. Peter's Church waiting for Gene Sr. and me to offer Jesus to him for the first time.

I prayed during that time to Mary, St. Joseph, Cardinal Cooke. The words "grace-filled moments" flooded my soul. Then Gene came and sat beside me. He placed his head on my shoulder. There are no books, no manuals, telling parents how to prepare your child for death, for heaven. I told Gene not to be afraid, that Jesus was with him and us. We talked about death and separation. I told him that I would always love him — that just as I had carried him *under* my heart for so many months that I would carry him forever *in* my heart. We also talked about how important it was to stay open to the will of God, and not to panic. He still said that he was convinced that God wanted him to be a priest. He also said that he was not afraid. We prayed together and then left to pick up Gene Sr.[1]

Margaret recalls that even then Gene's sense of humor did not leave him. Margaret easily got lost in the city. Suddenly they were driving by St. Patrick's Cathedral and Margaret said, "Now I know where I am." Gene laughed and with his dry sense of humor answered, "You may know where you are now, but you sure don't know where you are going!"[2]

They picked up Gene Sr. and shared the news with him, and then immediately drove to Suffern to see their friend and local oncologist who had supervised Gene's treatment at Good Samaritan, Dr. Sushil Bhardwaj. This good friend was as positive as he could be and discussed various possibilities, including radiation. This positive attitude did much to help Gene.

Margaret reports that the three then went home to bring the news to Tom and that evening drove to St. Joseph's Seminary to share the news with Bishop O'Brien. While Gene and the Bishop spoke, Margaret recalls that the rest of the family sat in the chapel:

> We prayed to Cardinal Cooke, who had sat in that same chapel as a seminarian only fifty years earlier. "Please help us, Cardinal Cooke." The words "grace-filled moments" [Cardinal Cooke's expression for his own acceptance of terminal cancer] kept racing through my mind. When Gene and Bishop O'Brien reappeared at the door of the chapel, I remember repeating those words aloud. We left the seminary, and as we did Gene told us that he had asked Bishop O'Brien about the possibility of moving candidacy up.[3]

Living Each Day to the Fullest

Despite the darkness, the next weeks were also filled with some bright light. People who have feared a terminal diagnosis and then receive it are often relieved to be free from the suspense. Their road is clear — especially if they are believers. They are clearly now in the Hands of God. There is no time to waste. Every day must be lived to the fullest. Although Margaret did not realize this at the time, her account of those few weeks has a certain peace about it, a peace that reflected the peace of her dying son:

> During the following days we decided that very few people would be told the entire story. Gene was adamant about the point that this period of time was a time of living, of life. He didn't want the next few months to become a wake. Therefore, aside from the immediate fam-

ily only Cardinal O'Connor, Bishop O'Brien, Monsignor Sullivan, Father Barrett, Father Derivan, Monsignor Farley, Father Charles Kelly, and Michael Martine and Frank Bassett knew the full story.

During the week of June twenty-fourth, Gene started radiation treatment at Good Samaritan, five days a week. We often combined this with a holy hour, or "spiritual radiation therapy," at the hospital chapel. Gene kept to a routine. We said Morning Prayer and Rosary together before going to the hospital. Following the holy hour we went to twelve o'clock Mass at the Marian Shrine. During the afternoon, Gene read and rested. Evening Prayer and Night Prayer were said with Gene Sr. or Frank Bassett. During the summer months, Gene often spent another period of time before the Blessed Sacrament with his father at St. Peter's Church. On Wednesday nights he and Frank Bassett went up to the Marian Shrine for their holy hour. During the summer this continued even when chemotherapy was combined with the radiation.

On July fourth, we had a special family day together. We asked Gene where he would like to go, and he said Philadelphia. When his classmates had visited the Neumann Shrine, Gene had been sick. He wanted to pray at the Shrine of St. John Neumann. We had a wonderful time both there and traveling. Later, in the summer, we made another trip back there the weekend before Gene went to Dunwoodie. When we returned from the Neumann Shrine we had a message on our answering machine from Bishop O'Brien. He told us that candidacy would be on Saturday, July sixth, in his chapel.

On July fifth, we were granted a special favor. We were allowed to go down into the crypt at St. Patrick's Cathedral and pray at the tomb of Cardinal Cooke. After praying there as a family and ending our prayers with the *Salve Regina*, Gene remained behind to pray alone.

July sixth: a beautiful day in more ways than one. By [bestowing] candidacy, the Church recognized that Gene had a vocation and promised to do everything to nurture it. Bishop O'Brien was the main celebrant. Father Barrett called Gene forth. Monsignors Sullivan and Farley concelebrated. It was a happy day. The celebration continued after Mass in the dining room. We laughed and had a wonderful time, something we hadn't done in a long time. We didn't know it then, but a week later Father Barrett would be called home to the Lord.[4]

Those Who Go Before the Dying

The death of Father Brian Barrett, which was already discussed, deeply affected Gene, because he now considered himself as one of the dying. After the funeral Gene remembered, "I shall really, really miss him. But he died a priest."[5] Immediately after Father Barrett's death, Gene's Confirmation sponsor, his mother's best friend Ann MacDonald, also died of cancer. Gene had spent hours with her and they had become very close. Again Gene was reminded that he was on his journey alone. Perhaps he had begun to question what often occurs to people in a terminal situation when someone dies before them. Which is the more real world, this one or where we are all going? Despite the fact that he knew that his days were numbered, Gene began to experience — this is the most accurate word to describe it — the conviction that he was going to be a priest. Margaret writes:

While there was a certain sadness about Gene after the death of these two important people in his life, his demeanor was marked with a quiet determination. He seemed to have a sense of purpose. It was at this time that the concept of ordination as the Will of God for him began to take center stage in his life. He prayed for ordination because he felt it was God's Will for him. He prayed for healing if it was God's Will.[6]

A Gentle Calm Before the Storm

During that summer, Monsignor Farley, the spiritual director of St. Joseph's, came regularly to the Hamilton home every week and offered Mass, and he gave Gene an opportunity for spiritual direction and confession. Gene actually was feeling better. It was a gentle calm before the storm. Despite all, life went on and with it the hope of ordination. We can sense this hope in Margaret's account:

> Gene was determined to return to Dunwoodie at the end of August for the retreat and workshops. The tumor markers were dropping. The CAT scans and X rays looked good. He returned after Labor Day. For the first time, I heard Gene say that he had to pace himself. He was assigned Father Giandurco as his academic advisor. Father Giandurco was a gift to Gene. He was Ann MacDonald's cousin, and Gene established an easy rapport with him. Also Father Sorgie, academic dean, realized that Gene was seriously ill and urged Gene to pace himself as well. Gene did drop one course. During September, Gene never seemed better. He received the Ministry of Lector on September tenth. He continued on the chemo and saw Dr. Bhardwaj on a weekly basis.[7]

In September, Gene was hospitalized with pneumonia related to his low blood-count. During this time and the period of recovery, he kept up his studies and went back to his old prayer routine with his parents. He was, however, able to return to Dunwoodie. It was at this time, a week before Thanksgiving, that Monsignor Farley assisted him in formulating and taking the vow of celibacy which would so providentially prepare for the gift and mystery that was to come. Margaret remarks that Thanksgiving Day "was truly a day of thanksgiving for all of us."[8] The reader may find these words puzzling. How little it takes to make someone grateful who has so very little to hope for in this world. That sense of gratitude is linked with profound faith and love of God. The Advent and Christmas seasons this year were filled with gratitude by Gene and his family. Unknown to Gene, the first steps were being taken toward a request to the Holy Father for permission to ordain him to the priesthood.

The Thoughts of Youth Are Long Thoughts

We need to interrupt our narrative at this crucial point because we need to ask, What was going on in Gene's mind during all these months? As the old Irish saying reminds us, his thoughts were long thoughts. His mother has provided us with a deeply moving narrative sprinkled with Gene's own revealing words. He had begun working on his own book. But before we move on to the final days of Gene's life, we need to pause and look beneath the external events. With all that we have seen so far, you will be deeply moved, and I hope you will be changed (as I was changed) by what Gene Hamilton wrote at this time — as he was beginning his book entitled *Servant, Victim, Brother, Listener, Friend.*

These reflections will form the basis for the rest of my outlook towards the disease, life, death, the priesthood, and others. One could say they are the lens through which I look at cancer and the overall experience. . . .

My hope is that all those affected by this disease — the patients, families, friends, and those who care for them, will come to a certain amount of peace in their own particular situation. I have found such peace in the Will of the Father. That is where the seminarian and future priest will himself find peace as well. Cardinal Cooke realized this and chose *Fiat Voluntas Tua* ("Thy Will Be Done") as his episcopal motto. For those left behind for a while, my prayer is for your own peace as well. Rest assured, it is now my plea to the Lord for all eternity.[9]

A Model and Guide on the Way

Anyone living through terminal illness or being a loving friend walking this road with another is likely to feel that somehow God has failed them. Perhaps they can come to grips with this most obvious fact of life — that we are all here for a short time and that we are on a journey. The tennis star Arthur Ashe, who died of AIDS contracted from a blood transfusion, confessed that he first was haunted with the question "Why me?" and then, responding to the simple Bible Christianity of his youth in the South, he asked himself, "Why not me?" This is an important step. But terminally ill people who have even gotten this far may feel that God has forgotten them. Often this is because they fail to recognize and embrace the help that God is in fact sending them at this time. Clergy and medical personnel often watch with sadness and frustration as the sick push away the very grace-filled opportunities they have refused to use in their struggle to make sense out of death and be prepared to meet God.

Not Eugene! He characteristically recognized that he was receiving much support and help beginning with his own family and the many friends he had in the Church. But all these people, except for his fellow patients with cancer, stood outside of his special world of the dying. However, perhaps for our benefit more than for his own, God provided a special guide and friend, someone who had made the journey before, Terence Cardinal Cooke. In his book, Gene sums up his personal relationship with Cardinal Cooke in a deeply moving way:

> There was an individual who seemed to do better in the abandonment and surrender categories than I did. He became a model for me, for his whole life was an active seeking of the Will of God and a willingness to carry that out, regardless of the circumstances.
>
> Terence J. Cooke, Archbishop of New York, became a model for my struggle with cancer and a model for my vocation. For [nineteen] years, Cardinal Cooke battled cancer and lived out his priestly vocation. His perseverance was admirable; his fidelity to his personal understanding of a priest was remarkable. Both were qualities that I had come to admire many years before I myself became sick.
>
> My father had been ordained a permanent deacon by Cardinal Cooke in 1982, a little over a year before the Cardinal died. My brother and I were very young at the time and the Cardinal took great care to be attentive to our excitement at meeting someone like him. This was my only encounter with the man while he was alive. I watched his funeral on TV a year later, while the City and Archdiocese of New York mourned their loss. John Cardinal O'Connor, Cardinal Cooke's successor as Archbishop of New York, began the process by which he [Cardinal Cooke]

is now being considered for canonization (saint-hood).

I had thought of Cardinal Cooke often in my seminary years and the preceding years while I was contemplating my vocation. His episcopal motto, *Fiat Voluntas Tua* ("Thy Will Be Done"), highlighted my own desire to do the Will of the Father. Throughout my life it was the Father's Will that had drawn me in directions and led me to follow paths that I never would have dreamed of. In the course of trying to follow the Father's Will in my life I had encountered many friends and others whom I came to admire, appreciate, and thank the Lord for bringing into my life. I used to laugh when others would wonder what I would do with my life. I laughed even more when people found out I was going into the seminary. They seemed to think I might go "here," or become pastor of "there," or be in charge of "this," or even be head of "that." Many of the suggestions, while flattering, had nothing to do with the essence of the priesthood. They were secondary to my vocation and to why I was entering the seminary. After realizing I had cancer, I became convinced that God's Will was definitely more varied than imaginations of well-wishers. I had committed myself to following His Will; now I would have to live out that commitment.

While it is true that those who are exploring their vocation in life have as a motive the Will of God, discerning that Will is the hard part. Prior to getting sick, I struggled in discernment, wondering if this was the proper way God wanted me to use the gifts He had given me. After receiving the diagnosis of cancer, I was faced with a life-threatening illness. I had to face death, and in facing death, I had to face life. I was fortunate in that I was able to say that being on the road to priesthood was where God wanted me to be in my life at that moment. Where cancer fit into that was another matter. Yet, these reflections perhaps can shed some light upon the question.

With my diagnosis, I became more familiar with the life of Cardinal Cooke and the man himself by reading everything I could on him. I would speak with him in prayer; he had cancer, he would understand. I would tell him of how much I wanted to be a priest, and I got a sense of his own love of the priesthood. While I would receive my chemotherapy treatments, I would whisper *"Fiat Voluntas Tua"* over and over. It became my prayer and my hope. Like a true saint, he drew me closer to God, to Mary, and to the Church. I asked one and all to pray for the Cardinal's intercession and his ultimate canonization. Here was a New York priest with cancer, this was an individual who would realize what I was going through. My relationship with Cardinal Cooke brought me out of this physical world, yet the situation became more real. I was praying with and asking the intercession of someone in the spiritual world, yet I became more human as a result. My connection with Cardinal Cooke never took me out of this world but firmly planted me in it. After receiving my terminal diagnosis, I went to the crypt in St. Patrick's Cathedral to visit Cardinal Cooke's tomb. After praying with my family, I spent some time alone in that crypt. With each passing day, I was being drawn closer to him; the Father's Will had become more urgent. Like Cardinal Cooke, I had now entered that mysterious category of persons known as the dying.[10]

It is poignant to recall that in November 1996, two months before his death, I suggested to Gene that we visit the crypt where Cardinal Cooke is buried under the high altar in the cathedral. He never mentioned to me that he had made this visit earlier with his family. Monsignor Farley and I prayed with Gene and then we quietly withdrew. The upright figure of this young man kneeling a few inches from the tomb will always be vividly in my mind. Having often prayed to the Cardinal myself, I never felt closer to him than I did that day. There have been a number of reports of cures from terminal illness through the Cardinal's intercession — even of people closer to death than Eugene was that day — particularly a young girl from New Jersey who was at death's door with AML leukemia, which disappeared in two hours. I recall whispering as we came up the stairs from the crypt, "Come on, Terry, you have to do something for this kid." I walked quickly because I did not want Gene to see my tears. Actually I was to discover when I taped my interview with him a month later that Cardinal Cooke's intercession had been very productive. Gene commented, ". . . I think people as a result of the example of Cardinal Cooke and learning more about him probably have a greater acceptance and understanding of God's Will in their own life. And that was something that was not just an episcopal motto for him in terms of 'Thy Will Be Done,' but it became a way of life and a way of living, not just for him but now for others as well."[11] Gene was, I am sure, speaking also about himself and the reactions of others to his impending death.

Salvifici Doloris

In the outline for the unfinished book, the third chapter has this Latin title, taken from the apostolic letter of Pope John

Paul II, *On the Christian Meaning of Human Suffering*, February 11, 1984. Gene obviously meant to dedicate this chapter to applying the teachings and experience of this great pope to his own life. We have only this outline to go by in order to guess what the chapter might have told us:

> Theology of human suffering from personal perspective; salvific meaning; spiritual sacrifice and unification; identification with the Cross; pain and suffering; curing and healing. . . .[12]

When I interviewed Gene on December 27, 1996, he spoke explicitly about *Salvifici Doloris* and related this letter to Cardinal O'Connor:

> The Cardinal has always been very, very gracious to me and even from the first awareness of my illness he's called many times to see how I'm doing. It was Cardinal O'Connor who highlighted the importance and the connection between priesthood and the understanding of human suffering and the salvific meaning that it takes on. In many ways I've been influenced by John Paul II's 1984 Apostolic Letter on the salvific meaning of human suffering, *Salvifici Doloris*. But it's been Cardinal O'Connor in many ways who has helped me to make that document, make those words very, very practical and very, very lived out. And so he's highlighted the importance and the supernatural value that suffering can take on and he's shown by his own example the importance that has for the priesthood itself, how the priest himself (as Cardinal Cooke highlighted) may sometimes be called to be a co-victim with Our Lord and to conform himself to our Lord

Jesus even on the Cross. And so I guess Cardinal O'Connor has made all of that very, very real by his words of encouragement and by his constant guidance and concern for my own particular case.[13]

Later, when we explore Gene's own personal view of the priesthood we will return to the concept of a priest as victim. Space does not permit us a thorough summary of *Salvifici Doloris*, which is a deeply personal restatement of a profound Christian theme in concepts relevant to the times in which we live. The letter was issued during the Holy Year of the Redemption, marking the nineteen hundred and fiftieth anniversary of the death and resurrection of Christ. In the final paragraphs of the apostolic letter, the Pope summarizes this teaching in a way that obviously is meaningful to any person who is undergoing physical suffering or psychological anguish:

> The mystery of the Redemption of the world is in an amazing way rooted in suffering, and this suffering in turn finds in the mystery of the Redemption its supreme and surest point of reference.
>
> We wish to live this Year of Redemption in special union with all those who suffer. And so there should come together in spirit beneath the Cross of Calvary all suffering people who believe in Christ, and particularly those who suffer because of their faith in Him who is the crucified and risen One, so that the offering of their sufferings may hasten the fulfillment of the prayer of the Savior Himself that all may be one. Let there also gather beneath the Cross all people of good will, for on this Cross is the "Redeemer of man," the Man of Sorrows, who has taken upon Himself the physical and moral sufferings of

the people of all times, so that in love they may find the salvific meaning of their sorrow and valid answers to all of their questions.[14]

The Holy Father clearly intended by this personal document to refocus the attention of believers on an essential aspect of Christianity which is in danger of being lost in a world of naturalism and hedonism. The modern world does everything possible to avoid suffering and pain but paradoxically often experiences more psychic pain than those who must with dignity live with their pain. According to the pope Christ's willing acceptance of the Cross is a model for all who suffer since out of that acceptance He fashioned the salvation of the world and the defeat of evil.

The Cross at the Center

The theme of suffering willingly with Christ is so far removed from many contemporary values that some readers may find it almost incomprehensible. This is sad because suffering sooner or later is the experience of all. It was Archbishop Fulton Sheen who commented that there was nothing worse than wasted suffering. The following quotation from Cardinal Newman, although in Victorian English, eloquently locates the place of the Cross in the Christian's understanding and acceptance of suffering:

> Ten thousand things come before us one after another in the course of life, and what are we to think of them? what colour are we to give them? Are we to look at all things in a gay and mirthful way? or in a melancholy way? in a desponding or a hopeful way? Are we to make light of life altogether, or to treat the whole subject seriously? Are we to make greatest things of little consequence,

or least things of great consequence? Are we to keep in mind what is past and gone, or are we to look to the future, or are we to be absorbed in what is present? How are we to look at things? this is the question which all persons of observation ask themselves, and answer each in his own way. They wish to think by rule; by something within them, which may harmonize and adjust what is without them. Such is the need felt by reflective minds. Now, let me ask, what is the real key, what is the Christian interpretation of this world? What is given us by revelation to estimate and measure this world by? Crucifixion of the Son of God.

It is the death of the Eternal Word of God made flesh which is our great lesson how to think and how to speak of this world. His Cross has put its due value upon every thing which we see, upon all fortunes, all advantages, all ranks, all dignities, all pleasures; upon the lust of the flesh, and the lust of the eyes, and the pride of life. It has set a price upon the excitements, the rivalries, the hopes, the fears, the desires, the efforts, the triumphs of mortal man. It has given a meaning to the various, shifting course, the trials, the temptations, the sufferings, of his earthly state. It has brought together and made consistent all that seemed discordant and aimless. It has taught us how to live, how to use this world, what to expect, what to desire, what to hope. It is the tone into which all the strains of this world's music are ultimately to be resolved. . . .

. . . They alone are able truly to enjoy this world who begin with the world unseen. They alone enjoy it who have first abstained from it. . . . They alone inherit it who take it as a shadow of the world to come, and who for that world to come relinquish it.[15]

We are about to read an account of sorrow, discouragement, and pain, borne with hope and even cheerfulness. We will see a young man with many talents and gifts, more than most of us, walk into a blinding storm of pain and suffering and not lose his way. Although he will be supported by a loving family and friends, he must, as we all must, walk through the valley of the shadow of death by himself. Only the Good Shepherd can accompany us. If you seek to really understand how Gene did this, it will be a most valuable lesson to learn, but you must keep in mind that he saw all things in the light of the Cross of Jesus Christ.

Endnotes

1. Diary of Margaret Hamilton, 9-11.
2. Ibid., 12.
3. Ibid., 13.
4. Ibid., 14-16.
5. Ibid., 16.
6. Ibid., 17.
7. Ibid., 17-18.
8. Ibid., 20.
9. *Servant, Victim, Brother, Listener, Friend*, 7-8. This manuscript hereafter referred to as *Servant*.
10. Ibid., 9-10.
11. December 27, 1996, Interview, 8.
12. Servant, 1.
13. December 27, 1996, Interview, 8.
14. *On the Christian Meaning of Human Suffering* (Boston: St. Paul Editions), no. 31, pp. 55-56.
15. *Parochial and Plain Sermons*, vol. 6, sermon 7, "The Cross of Christ the Measure of the World," excerpted in *The Heart of Newman*, ed. Erich Przywara, S.J. (San Francisco: Ignatius Press, 1997), 325-326.

7

Preparation for Priesthood...

...Preparation for Death

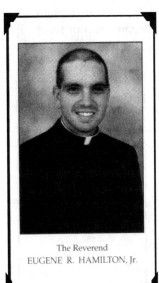

The Reverend
EUGENE R. HAMILTON, Jr.

This startling chapter heading is so painful to read that I would never have thought of using it, except that it is the title that Gene gives to Chapter Five of the book he never completed. He adds in the outline: "Compatibility of the two concepts; need to reflect upon the essentials; importance of prioritization."[1] These words, with their startling contrast, were to come to an incredible conclusion when the ordination cards of Father Eugene Hamilton became also the memorial cards of his death. He had designed these himself and left them in his computer.

If there were ever cards like these ordination/death cards issued in the history of the Catholic Church, no one has ever been able to find an example. Although the singular nature of Gene's ordination is not the important issue, one must thoughtfully pause when one reads the title he proposed for the fifth chapter of his autobiography.

We need to spend some time delving into Gene's own personal concept of the priesthood. We know that he saw the priest, as Cardinal Cooke had seen this role of the representative of Christ, as a servant, victim, brother, listener, and friend. In our December interview Gene said:

> . . . Those five categories, those five traits have been something that I had hoped and still hope to be able to emulate as priest. They are also five goals that I as a seminarian am trying to form and trying to move towards in the vocation that I believe God is calling me to. In a very real sense I guess one can try to live out and try to work through those five categories so they become sort of focal points. This is so that I can ask myself the ques-

In Prayerful Remembrance of

The Reverend
EUGENE R. HAMILTON, Jr.
Born October 29, 1972
Ordained January 24, 1997
Died January 24, 1997

ANIMA CHRISTI

Soul of Christ, make me holy.
Body of Christ, be my salvation.
Blood of Christ, let me drink Your wine.
Water flowing from the side of Christ,
wash me clean.
Passion of Christ, strengthen me.
Kind Jesus, hear my prayer;
hide me within Your wounds
and keep me close to You.
Defend me from the evil enemy.
Call me at my death
to the fellowship of Your saints,
that I may sing Your praise with them
through all eternity. Amen.

T. J. McGOWAN SONS, Inc.
Funeral Directors
133 Broadway, Haverstraw, NY

In Prayerful Remembrance of

The Reverend
EUGENE R. HAMILTON, Jr.
Born October 29, 1972
Ordained January 24, 1997
Died January 24, 1997

"From the day of his ordination, a priest can never forget that he has been called by God Himself. The priest is called to be.

a Servant...
...a Victim...
...a Brother...
...a Listener...
...a Friend...

The anointing that Jesus gives us is to help us bring Him into our world..."
Terence Cardinal Cooke

T. J. McGOWAN SONS, Inc.
Funeral Directors
133 Broadway, Haverstraw, NY

There were two ordination/death cards for Father Gene.

tion, how have I served the Lord today? How have I united my sufferings with him for others, so that they can take on salvific meaning and that good can come out of a not-so-good situation? How have I been a brother to others? How have I been a friend to those who do not have a friend? And have I listened to the Lord and have I listened to Him through His Church? Have I accepted and been obedient to Him? Have I listened to Him through His word in Scripture? And have I listened to Him through other people? And that has to be done in a spirit of interior silence. And so my understanding of the priesthood is now definitely shaped. Some may say it's very practical or pragmatic to outline it by those five categories of servant, victim, brother, listener, and friend. Yet at the same time they are really a call to make sure that my whole person is always involved in carrying out what I believe to be God's will; that my whole person is always open to whatever that will of God is, whether I live or whether I die.[2]

We can only project how Father Eugene Hamilton would have lived out this ideal — by looking at how the many facets of the priesthood shaped his life as he worked to become a priest. Although we can find aspects of all these facets even in his high school career, it is in his last year-and-a-half that we see him wrestling with illness and trying to live out this priestly role as a seminarian. These eighteen months give us the best insights into his life as it was and into what it might have become.

Love Does Not Fail

It is important to bear in mind as we examine the last year-and-a-half of Gene's life that the step after faith and hope on the spiritual journey is charity or love, first of neighbor and then rising in a crescendo to an ever more powerful love of God. Love was defined by St. Thomas Aquinas as the giving away of itself — *bonum est defusium sui*. This love is the very being of God. Love is what we know best of this most mysterious and transcendent Being from whom we come and to whom we hope to return. God is love (1 John 4:16). In the life of Our Lord and all the saints we see that holiness is love and that the real fruit of faith and hope is love — for others and for God. You will only be able to make some sense out of the life of Eugene Hamilton and his ideal of the Christian life lived in the priesthood if you understand that this dying young man saw the priest as a servant of love.

Servant

The idea that being a servant is not something to be despised or avoided was unique to Christ's Gospel in the ancient world. Our Lord reveals that He is among us as "Him who serves." The Mass of Holy Thursday with the washing of the feet is also the actual anniversary of the priesthood and the Eucharist. Unfortunately, there are sad examples in Church history of clergy who saw their role as that of the lord of the manor, and even popes who forgot that one of the titles of the successors of Peter is "Servant of the Servants of God." St. Augustine, in an ordination sermon of another bishop, tells us that all ordained in the name of Christ must learn from Christ, who teaches us from the podium of the Cross, and that they are to be true to the model of the serving Savior.[3] Candidates for the priesthood respond to their liturgical call by saying, "I have come to serve."

Gene, following the humble servant of God Terence Cardinal Cooke, saw the Christian as a servant, and especially aspired to the priesthood in this role. He clearly saw being a servant first as being a servant to God. He had always enjoyed being an altar server and later in high school a Eucharistic minister, and a sacristan at the college. Part of his responsibility at Manhattan College as sacristan was to see that the marriages of students and alumni were properly performed and recorded in the local parish of the Visitation. Monsignor Robert Larkin, the pastor, writes:

> In his role as the sacristan, Gene was very careful that the necessary arrangements were made for the proper celebration of any marriage scheduled to take place in the college chapel. He had a genuine respect for the Church and her teachings. Gene was concerned that the college chapel would always be used in a fitting manner and that marriages in the chapel were validly celebrated. . . .
>
> In the weeks since Gene's death, I have thought of Gene frequently. His courage, determination, patient endurance, and faith-filled trust continue to inspire me to strive to be more the kind of priest that Gene so wanted to be. His desire for priesthood and his determination to strive to work toward priestly ordination despite a life-consuming illness has provided me with fruitful meditations upon the gift of priesthood and the call to serve the Lord and His people generously, untiringly, and with deep trust that His will be done. I am confident that God, in His own way, will use the experience of knowing Eugene Hamilton — if only for a few brief years on this earth — to remind me frequently to rejoice in the gift of priesthood and to strive to extend myself very generously in priestly service, as I know Gene would have done. It was a great privilege to be inspired by Gene for so brief a time here on earth; it will be an even greater privilege to experience his intercession before the Father in the

fraternity of the priesthood of Jesus Christ in which we both now share.[4]

Gene also served others in so many capacities. Even when one visited him in his last days of illness he was concerned for the comfort of his guests, and when asked how he was doing would quickly but unobtrusively change the subject to his guests and their interests and well-being. This has been a constant theme in letters received from those who knew this book was in process.

Victim

As we have mentioned, this title is an intimidating one for many. When I asked Gene about his concept of victim in our December 1996 interview, his answer was most illuminating:

> For myself, I guess having grown up in the modern world I realize how much the word "victim" has been victimized even of itself. I guess it's an understanding, a realization that in the particular human condition that we're in, because of original sin, evil has entered the world. As a result of that we have human suffering, and yet at the same time we have hope because we've been redeemed by Jesus Christ. And He specifically chose the plan of God, that He would redeem the world through His suffering on the Cross and by dying and then rising to new life. And so it is through the passion, death, and resurrection that is re-presented in the Eucharistic sacrifice and that we proclaim in the Scriptures that we realize that it is in dying that we become born into eternal life. And so we've regained that life through the Cross of Christ through His resurrection. While we're on this pilgrimage here on earth, the Cross gives us a better

understanding of the fact that this is not the end, but it is merely a part of that pilgrimage towards our ultimate goal and what the Lord wants for us — eternal life with Him forever. And so I believe that those who suffer in this life can be assured that Jesus is very, very close to them in their suffering. That Jesus will always hold out his hand to them in their suffering and that He will be with them in their suffering and that they can unite that suffering with His on the Cross. Therefore suffering takes on that salvific meaning for the salvation of others so that merit and grace can be given for others. [It permits us] basically to take a very active role in God's plan of redemption.[5]

These words take on all the more meaning because they are spoken by a man who had suffered intensely for a year-and-a-half and who had lived through repeated appalling disappointments during his medical treatment. The very spiritual doctrine of the Cross on which Gene's words were built has come to be seen by many as trite, pietistic, or even masochistic. The following statement made on December 27, when Gene was already desperately ill and the hope of a cure was fading, should be read slowly and perhaps a few times. I had asked him in the interview about his feelings regarding the bleak medical reports he was getting:

I guess you could say those are the days where all you can really do is cling to that which is in front of you and yet also it disappears from your sight. And what you're clinging to is that Cross of Christ. When I say it disappears, the various events and the pain and the diagnostic reports or the bad test results that might come in seem to make that vision of the Cross more difficult to see. And yet

in your heart of hearts, in your very soul, you somehow know it's there and you somehow instinctively
reach out to it and try to hold on to it at the same
time, in an effort because you hope and pray that
stretching out on the other side is that hand of Jesus
and hopefully He is willing to take you into His
hand.[6]

Gene's spiritual director, Father Thomas Derivan, saw a very
special dimension of the victim in Gene's life. Perhaps Gene
was so close to all this that he did not see it or at least articu-
late it as sharply as his director did:

I always had the sense that Gene almost knew
that this was God's plan. It is almost as if he knew
something that we did not know, namely that in
him God was disclosing a new dimension of priesthood — perhaps not really new, but new in the
sense that we seldom talk of it. And this dimension was the dimension of the victim-sufferer, even
the victim-priest. In Gene, the Lord was painting
again the picture of Isaiah's Suffering Servant and
asking Gene to participate in a modern-day re-
enactment of that mystery. So often we think of
priesthood as our choice, our decision, our commitment. In Gene, the Lord was drawing us back
to His definition of priesthood, defined in the person of the Suffering Jesus. I think Gene knew that
he was a player in a divine drama that transcended
him, and that, in some way, was part of God's teaching us what the priesthood really is.[7]

Brother

One of the most appealing qualities of Gene's ideal, Terence
Cardinal Cooke, was that he saw himself as a brother to all. At

the time of the Cardinal's death members of practically every major ethnic group and religious affiliation in New York paid tribute to him as a brother concerned with all, especially the disadvantaged.[8]

Gene Hamilton was never in a position to do this, but early on in high school and college he showed himself concerned for his fellow students — and especially those in need. It was, however, when he became ill that this aspect of his personality really came into focus. In his brief description of Chapter Thirteen of the unfinished autobiography, entitled "Ministry of a Patient/Seminarian," he mentions the challenges his illness brought to him to live out his vocation even while he was dying:

> This is where I was called to live out my vocation, to be all of what God wanted of me in the particular situation. At times that may have seemed like everything; at other times it may have been nothing at all.
>
> Many people have been affected by me battling cancer.[9]

Actually we learn from Gene's family and friends that he spent much of his time in the hospital, especially in Memorial Hospital, visiting other patients and assisting them with their own fears and sorrows. He particularly befriended some of the younger patients at Memorial Sloan. Gene also spoke of making the Stations of the Cross while visiting his fellow patients and of identifying them with Christ in His Passion. He used the opportunity to pray specially for them that their sufferings would lead them to eternal life.

When I visited Gene the last few times I could only recall the visit I had paid to Cardinal Cooke a month before he died and the day before I had open heart surgery. I visited the Cardinal, who was by then unable to stand, at his residence, hoping to bring him some consolation. I blush now to think of this presumption, because he spent the precious hour making me feel better. Many have reported that they left their visit with this dying seminarian feeling sad but strangely consoled or at least spiritually more aware than they were when they arrived.

Listener

It was proverbial of Cardinal Cooke that he liked to go to meetings and that he usually let everybody else speak first. Considering that he attended two hundred meetings in the last eight months of his life while he was severely ill, he must be called very much a listener. Those who knew Gene in high school have said that he was always willing to stop and help a fellow student with lessons or any other need. His seminarian friends recall that when they visited while he was at home while sick, the conversation was always about how things were going at the seminary and what was happening. These conversations were never gossip, but rather reflected Gene's genuine concern for those with whom he felt a special bond even if they did not really know him well. He especially practiced the art of listening when he was with his suffering fellow patients. The motive for all this listening was the same motive that I know inspired Cardinal Cooke. The following lines taken from Gene's outline could have been written by the Cardinal himself. When I asked Gene if he felt Christ's presence in all that he experienced, his response was:

> Absolutely, and I guess you can say that I've felt His real presence in the various people that I've met over the course of this illness. You realize that you see Christ in the person who is suffering in the bed next to you and you see Christ in the doctors and the nurses who come in to take care of you when you yourself are helpless and unable to do so. Those are the times where that dynamic

relationship with Christ becomes all the more real and you realize that yes you may not be able to see Him but He's there.[10]

Friend

When Cardinal Cooke died, the Spanish-language newspaper in New York, *El Diario*, carried a beautiful portrait of him on the front page with the words "*Adios Amigo*" — "Goodbye, Friend."[11] Those who knew the Cardinal — or Gene — realized that they had great capacities for friendship, although paradoxically they were both rather private persons. Gene had many friends, and like the Cardinal he would say that it was his joyous vocation to be a friend to many — in the spiritual sense of a true friend. St. Augustine reminds us that someone is only a true friend if he helps us to come closer to God, our eternal good.

We have already considered Gene's time in college and his many friendships with students and faculty. The title "friend" gives us a most appropriate opportunity to look at Gene's attitude toward the seminary and toward formation. It is not a very well-kept secret that many an effective priest did not enjoy the seminary. This was especially true when seminaries were known for rigid discipline and when there was little or no apostolate for young men who had come with the goal of spreading the Gospel. But even in these days of more open programs and apostolic activities, one finds fine young priests who were very happy to say "Goodbye" to the seminary and get started in their apostolic and priestly life. Gene Hamilton was not one of these. Like his model, Cardinal Cooke, he loved the seminary and almost everything about it. He especially appreciated the teachers and became close friends with some of them: he valued friendships above all and he genuinely loved his fellow seminarians. The following quotation from our December interview struck me at the time I heard it as something Pope John Paul II might have said if he were talking to a group of seminarians. Gene seems to have forgotten that he was dying and would return only briefly to the seminary after the Christmas vacation:

> Being at the seminary really is somewhat of a dynamic relationship, not just between myself and God but also between myself and everybody else, whether that be my own classmates or whether that be the teachers in the classroom or whether they be the person who may be working there at that time. And so in a lot of ways I guess all of those experiences are coming together and all of those experiences are helping me move towards what I believe God is calling me to do. And somehow, in some way, the Lord wants me to interact with those individuals and to keep both my eyes and my ears open so that I can listen to His voice through others, so that I can listen to His voice through the Scriptures. It goes back, I think, to that whole atmosphere of formation and the importance of the seminary in that it is not just being a place of formation but an actual world of formation as well.[12]

To Remain Open

As we return to our narrative in the autumn before his death, we must recall that Gene knew he was terminally ill, and that he prayed either for a miraculous cure or for ordination to the priesthood. Gene had decided to begin the first year of theology in September 1996. Although he was having trouble seeing and reading because of chemotherapy, he kept up his studies. Frank Bassett highlighted some of the material for him so that he could take the exams. Gene feared that he would do badly, but in fact he did well. They joked about getting back to Gene's favorite pastime, miniature golf. They laughed about his favorite course that had a large giraffe in it, and they planned to go back there when he felt better.

Plans went on as if Gene were not terminally ill. This, in fact, is a wise procedure for those who are dying to follow as best they can. Gene intended to make himself available to be a priest — the rest was up to God. Along with his classmates he received the minor order of lector in the fall. Frank recalls that they made a prayer vigil the night before his receiving lector. Receiving orders while so ill had several purposes. Frank writes:

> To Gene, this acknowledgement was his way of telling the Church of a decision which he privately made to God. Gene and I also discussed the minor orders of lector and acolyte. We both agreed that these also were needed by seminarians. These were not to be taken lightly. They were commitments and graces would be received to continue toward ordination.[13]

Unknown to all, except perhaps confidentially to some of his spiritual advisors, in November Gene further pursued his vocation by making the private vow of celibacy, which we reproduced in Chapter Three.

Although only a few people knew he had received a terminal diagnosis, it was obvious that he was not doing well. Some asked why he was in the seminary, realizing that this was a great effort for him. I knew of these questions, and so I asked him directly during the December interview about why he was there:

> For me the seminary is not just a place, but it's really an atmosphere of formation. It's an atmosphere in which I'm called to grow closer to the Lord. Perhaps I stayed at the seminary for selfish reasons, because I know that the Lord is present

there in the Blessed Sacrament, and to have that easy access to the Lord in order to be with Him and pray with Him during the day and even, at times, at night. And at the same time I needed to be there in order to remain open to what the Lord was calling me to, what I believe to be a vocation to the priesthood, and also to be open to the human instruments that he uses, the rector and his faculty, my classmates and the others. And so the importance was there for my vocation, and also it was important in terms of what the Lord was calling me to. And that's where I felt God wanted me to be.[14]

The fact was, and Gene had told me this earlier, that he was hoping for a miraculous cure through the intercession of Cardinal Cooke and St. John Neumann, the humble and compassionate bishop of Philadelphia who was a special patron of his. He told me that he had a kind of intuition — a conviction that he would be a priest — and that this probably meant that he would either be cured or go into remission. This was not said in any fanatical way — but very gently, so as not to challenge me to believe it along with him unless I cared to do so. Somehow he knew he was to be a priest, and his stay at the seminary was an act of faith. It was early that December that a thought began to present itself to me — and to other people as well — that a dispensation should be sought so that he might be ordained a priest. Had he dropped out of the seminary, it is very doubtful if the move to obtain a dispensation would have ever started.

There were good institutional reasons for *not* seeking a dispensation. The Church can't ordain every seriously ill seminarian. Exceptions don't make good law. But canon law, unlike civil law, makes room for dispensations in exceptional cases. How in the world does one establish an exceptional case?

When asked about the possibility of Gene's early ordination Cardinal O'Connor replied, "Get me some facts."

But now we are getting ahead of our story.

Endnotes

1. *Servant, Victim, Brother, Listener, Friend*, 1. This autobiographical document hereafter referred to as *Servant*.
2. December 27, 1996 Interview, 5.
3. See Sermon 340A as given in *We Are Your Servants: Augustine on Ministry*, ed. Cardinal Michael Pellegrino (Philadelphia: Augustinian Press, 1986), 30-39.
4. Account of Monsignor Robert Larkin, March 23, 1997.
5. December 27, 1996, Interview, 8-9.
6. Ibid., 9.
7. Letter of Father Thomas Derivan to author, May 27, 1997.
8. See Father B. J. Groeschel, C.F.R. and Terence Weber, *Thy Will Be Done: A Spiritual Portrait of Terence Cardinal Cooke* (New York: Alba House, 1990).
9. *Servant*, 7.
10. December 27, 1996, Interview, 9.
11. Groeschel and Weber, *Thy Will Be Done*, 28.
12. December 27, 1996, Interview, 1-2.
13. Letter of Frank Bassett, May 30, 1997, 8.
14. December 27, 1996, Interview, 1.

8

The Cross at Christmas

Tom and Gene

Christmas is a strange holiday. It is not only the liturgical commemoration of the birth of our Savior; it also represents an attempt by the ancient Church to baptize the winter holiday of pagan times. Coupled with the haunting beauty of Advent and the supernatural joy of the Nativity of the Son of God in the humblest of circumstances, with the contrast of angels and shepherds, there is all the noise and tinsel of the winter solstice. It is a very difficult thing to be poor at Christmas, and even more trying to be very ill. When a dear one is very ill, or deeply disturbed, or in danger in military combat, or undergoing some deep catastrophe, this holiday can be very bitter indeed. To be dying at Christmas is a mystery all its own. Christmas celebrations may cruelly accent one's isolation from the rejoicing crowd. But when one has been blessed with firm faith and understands the reason of the Emmanuel's birth among us, then Christmas can have a special depth known only to those who see the shadow of the Cross over the Manger. During the Second World War the English spiritual writer Caryll Houselander summarized this mysterious conflict of joy and sorrow in a book with the striking title *The Passion of the Infant Christ*.[1] She reminded her wartime readers that even when Christ was born, the dark aspects of human existence were around Him. His family fled for their lives as refugees. He was desperately poor. The Cross was always there in the life of Jesus Christ.

The shadow of the Cross fell over the Hamiltons and their friends at Christmas of 1996. Margaret recalls those days of joy and sorrow, of life and impending death:

> In early December . . . after his hospital stay, Gene spent the next four days preparing to return to Dunwoodie. He read and completed some end-of-the-term assignments. A doctor's visit on December 12 indicated that Gene needed to return to Good Samaritan Hospital for treatment the following week. After a discussion with Bishop O'Brien and Father Giandurco, it was decided that Gene would return home with us on December 14 after the organ dedication recital. He spent the next two days completing take-home tests and other work for his classes.
>
> The December 17 to 19 cycle of treatments went as usual. Gene came home to rest because he

was determined to go to Midnight Mass at St. Peter's. Those days before Christmas were spent mostly in prayer, reading, resting, and planning Christmas presents.

Midnight Mass was the high point of our Christmas celebration. Despite his physical appearance, there was a certain strength and peace about Gene that evening. He was always comfortable and "at home" in the sanctuary during liturgical celebrations. This night was no different. As master of ceremonies, Gene didn't draw attention to himself. Rather, by seeing that all went smoothly, he directed attention to the altar where the Word became present.

When we arrived home, we checked to see if the Masses from St. Peter's in Rome and St. Patrick's Cathedral in New York City had been taped. We all sat and watched part of Pope John Paul II's Mass before retiring. . . .

Christmas Day itself was spent quietly and on Gene's time. We exchanged gifts with the sound of Christmas carols in the background. Gene's gifts for us were perfect. For Deacon Gene, two books — *First Lady of the World* by Father Peter Lappin, S.D.B., and *The Image of Mercy* by Bishop Emilio Allue. For Tom, the compact disc "A Sacred Treasury of Music," produced by Father Anthony Sorgie and the Dunwoodie choir. For me, a gold rose pin (the petals were red), a symbol of life. Gene was really moved by two of our gifts. One was a picture of his classmates taken when they graduated from the St. John Neumann Residence last June. The other was a picture of Mary Immaculate Seminary in Northampton, Pennsylvania, that was given to Gene by Father Brian Barrett. We had both of

these pictures framed. Gene always enjoyed opening the little gifts in his stocking. This Christmas
was no different. I remember looking at Gene as
he sat next to Tom, under the brightly lighted
Christmas tree. I could also see the ornament of
Humpty Dumpty that my parents had given him
on his first Christmas twenty-four years earlier. I
wondered, Is this Christmas Gene's last here?
Quickly, I got up and left the room to continue
preparing for dinner.

Gene had picked the menu — fruit cup, turkey,
mashed potatoes, corn, rolls, and pies. Frank
Bassett, Gene's classmate, joined us for dessert
and stayed until the next day. There were phone
calls from relatives and friends. A beautiful day!

The next day, December 26, was spent having
blood work done and working on the computer.
Gene had told me earlier that he was writing a
book. Gene was also collecting his thoughts for
his visit on December 27 with Father Benedict,
who was in the process of writing a book about
the priesthood and wished to interview Gene.

December 27 is our wedding anniversary. Both
of our sons wanted to make the day special. There
were flowers, a gift certificate for dinner, and a
perpetual spiritual enrollment.[2]

As a result of good financial planning and funds earned by
splendid Christmas concerts, the faculty and students of
Dunwoodie were able to visit Rome during the Christmas holiday. It was the second time. The obvious purpose of this grand
undertaking was to help the students have a better grasp of the
Universal Church — and especially of the role and primacy of
the Bishop of Rome. A great deal of personal loyalty to Pope
John Paul II, who had visited Dunwoodie in the fall of 1995,

made this visit an unusual and inspiring event. In fact, Gene had mentioned to me the possibility of asking the Holy Father's permission personally for him to be ordained ahead of time. Since I knew that such a petition was being contemplated, I suggested that a direct request might not be the best possible thing to do. I recalled to him the visit of St. Thérèse of Lisieux to Pope Leo XIII, and her directly asking permission to enter the Carmel before the canonical age. That request was not granted. Gene and I talked about some other possibilities. I did not tell him that some of us who knew him were in the process of inquiring about a dispensation.

Margaret continues the description of the events that happened after I left:

> Gene sat down with us and stated that he wanted to go to Rome with the seminarians on January 1. The hope was that if Pope John Paul II could meet him, then he might be more likely to grant permission to ordain him. Gene Sr. and I were very concerned because we didn't feel that Gene was up to this trip.[3]

At this point Gene's father came up with a good idea. Being a deacon and more familiar with the workings of the Church, he felt that his idea obviously had great merit and would produce a result quite beyond all his hopes. Deacon Hamilton writes:

> I suggested to him that he write a letter to the Pope asking for his prayers and that he send along his picture and a second picture of Gene at my ordination as a deacon to make the letter more personal. Gene agreed to do this. I also suggested that he ask Bishop O'Brien to take it personally to the Pope. The following Monday [December 30],

I drove Gene to the seminary where he gave his letter to the Pope to Bishop O'Brien along with the pictures. This gave all of us another small sense of hope, which is all we had.[4]

Gene's letter to the Holy Father, which was delivered by Bishop O'Brien, is deeply moving although rather formally written as one might expect. There is no doubt that the Holy Father read between the lines — as he must be accustomed to doing:

January 1, 1997
Solemnity of Mary, Mother of God

HIS HOLINESS JOHN PAUL II
Apostolic Palace
Vatican City State

Your Holiness,

Since September 1995, I have been suffering from a cancerous tumor in my chest cavity. In April 1996, I was operated upon to remove the tumor. In the month of June 1996, multiple cancerous tumors were discovered in the chest cavity and I was given a terminal diagnosis.

I ask for your prayers for the miracle of a complete recovery through the intercession of the Servant of God Terence Cardinal Cooke, with the assistance of Mary, Mother of the Church and Mother of Priests, and St. Joseph, Patron of the Universal Church, so that I may be ordained a priest to serve the Lord's people in the Archdiocese of New York.

Know that I unite my sufferings with those of our Lord Jesus Christ on the Cross, for the intentions of Your Holiness, and for priestly vocations to lead the Church into the third millennium.

With gratitude for your own priestly example, I am,

Respectfully yours in Christ,

> Eugene R. Hamilton, Jr.
> Class of 2000
> St. Joseph's Seminary
> Archdiocese of New York

Gene had prepared a youngster to be an altar boy for the first time at New Year's Eve Mass, which they attended. Frank Bassett spent New Year's Eve with the Hamiltons. There must have been many unspoken thoughts when the usual but subdued New Year's greetings were exchanged. What would 1997 bring? Frank left the next morning with all the seminarians for Rome, but his thoughts were with his best friend who, instead of going with them, spent the next two days in the hospital receiving treatment. Gene rested the next week while the students were away, quietly praying, reading, and trying to heal. His single expressed goal was to regain his strength so as to be able to return to Dunwoodie when they all got home. These few days would be the last little retreat Gene would ever have in this world.

The ominous news came from Dr. Bhardwaj that the measurement of the tumor showed that it was growing again despite surgery and several kinds of chemotherapy. He ordered a CAT scan for January 10. Those who have been through the terminal illness of a loved one know that the most ominous news, the real announcement of approaching death, often arrives in the most understated way, like the request for another CAT scan. Actually it was the summons to Calvary — but it was as little noticed by others as the fact that Judas had abruptly left the Last Supper. Gene, the Hamiltons, and their closest friends were all on the Way of the Cross.

Endnotes

1. London: Sheed and Ward, 1942.
2. Diary of Margaret Hamilton, 18-20.
3. Ibid., 20.
4. Diary of Eugene Hamilton, Sr., 17.

9

The Final Days

Gene's Funeral Mass

The title of this chapter is painful and puzzling. How can a
believer say "final"? But what we are to describe are the intense and sorrowful last days of an earthly life — days of life
counted in twenty-four-hour periods, marked by light and darkness, dawn and dusk. After the final days of this Creation will
come a day with sunrise but no sunset. We who believe contemplate that day which eye has not seen nor ear heard. We can
only prepare for it by peering through the door at the end of
the road and learning all that we can from this event which St.

Francis called "Our sister the death of the body." Death is many things — a biological fact, a sorrow, at times life's greatest hurt, but most of all death is a mystery. Why? Because it leads to life, to everlasting life, which we can only contemplate here from a great distance and through darkness like some faraway star.

As I write, the words of St. Paul in his First Letter to the Corinthians, which has been a foundation of our Christian belief about death, keep running through my mind:

> Lo! I tell you a mystery. We shall not all sleep, but we shall all be changed, in a moment, in the twinkling of an eye, at the last trumpet. For the trumpet will sound, and the dead will be raised imperishable, and we shall be changed. . . . When the perishable puts on the imperishable, and the mortal puts on immortality, then shall come to pass the saying that is written: "Death is swallowed up in victory" (1 Corinthians 15:51-52, 54).

We are now to witness the mystery.

The Way of the Cross

Fortunately we have an account of Gene's death from the closest possible source — his parents. Margaret providentially continued to keep her gripping diary through these stress-filled days:

> Dr. Bhardwaj decided that a CAT scan was in order, so he scheduled one for January 10 at 8:00 a.m. An office visit was scheduled for later that afternoon. It was usual for Gene to have blood work done prior to seeing the doctor. While this was being done, Dr. Bhardwaj called me out into the hallway. He stated that he had looked at the CAT

scan and that "it didn't look good." He mentioned that the cancer had spread to the liver — there were three or four nodules and one might be benign. He also stated that there was one near the pulmonary artery. The doctor stated that he was "devastated." As I stood there, with a sickening feeling spreading through my body, I told Dr. Bhardwaj that he had to tell Gene. We had always been honest with each other, and we must continue to be honest. I did ask Dr. Bhardwaj how long he thought Gene might live, but he said he didn't know.

Gene and I waited a while in the outside waiting room. He looked good and was anxious to get back to Dunwoodie on Sunday. "Please, Mary, Mother of Priests, help us. Cardinal Cooke, please do something." Finally, we were shown an examining room. Dr. Bhardwaj came in and calmly explained the results of the CAT scan with Gene. Gene asked questions. He knew what the doctor was saying. Then they discussed options, one of which was to stop all future treatments and be made comfortable when the time came. Gene ruled this out. Dr. Bhardwaj said that he wanted to talk to some of his colleagues and that he had already talked to Dr. K. about radiation. He said that he would call Gene and let him know.

The same faith, courage, trust, and determination that I had seen in Gene so often during the past sixteen months was still there. We talked on the way home. I told him that I wished that I could take his place, so that he could live. Gene calmly stated that this was not possible. "You still have a job to do. You have to take care of the family." We talked about love. I told him how much I loved him. I told him that he taught me how to love in a way that I had never loved before . . . I told him that he taught me what mother's love was all about. I repeated what I had said to him in June, that I would always hold him in my heart.

For the first time in over a year I became aware that Gene was probably not going to be physically healed. Gene was going to die.[1]

Anyone who has lived through the terminal illness of a loved one can easily recall the desperateness of the situation. The dying person is already on his journey, going down the road quickly, looking at the world from a perspective that the rest of us cannot share. Sometimes the dying remark that it is easier to be in their position than to be one of the helpless loved ones who are watching. Many believers at this time think of the Mother of Jesus going along the Via Dolorosa, standing on the sidelines with a broken heart. The Hamiltons were there, and as always they turned to prayer. Margaret continues:

The next ten days were probably the lowest I had ever gotten during his illness. Gene Sr. and I decided to go to Philadelphia on January 11 to pray at the shrine of St. John Neumann. We hardly spoke, except to cry. The thought of not having Gene with us was unbearable. What about Tom? They weren't just brothers. They were best friends. Every night, they talked on the phone when apart. When they were home, we would often be awakened at three in the morning by sounds of laughter. We stayed at the shrine for three hours. I prayed as I had prayed for so long — "Please, Jesus, let him live until he is ordained." We didn't know it then, but while we were at the St. John Neumann shrine a fax requesting dispensations that would allow an early ordination was being sent from New York to Rome.[2]

This fax from Cardinal O'Connor personally requesting permission to ordain Gene three-and-a-half years before the completion of his studies was sent to Cardinal Pio Laghi, Prefect of the Congregation for Catholic Education. Cardinal Laghi had often been to Dunwoodie and had made many friends in New York, including Cardinal O'Connor and Bishop O'Brien, when he was Apostolic Pro-Nuncio to the United States. He, in fact, had sufficient authority to grant the dispensation himself. Nonetheless, he decided to include the Holy Father in this process. As we shall see, this unrequired involvement of the

Gene's picture signed personally by Pope John Paul II.

Holy Father would prove to be a very providential aspect of the unique circumstances of Gene's ordination.

A Last Light Moment

It often happens in a terminal situation that the ordinary flow of life emerges incongruously. The dying tell jokes. Everyone laughs and forgets for a few moments. It is really a providential aspect of human behavior; otherwise our ability to function might be overwhelmed. Such an interlude occurred. Gene's good friend Frank Bassett arrived back from Rome about the same hour that the Hamiltons drove back from the shrine of St. John Neumann.

Everyone was delighted with Frank's stories of the trip to Rome. Gene especially was thrilled and moved to receive the letter from Pope John Paul II signed by his corresponding secretary and the personally signed picture. The Pope had returned both Gene's pictures with a letter saying that he would pray for them:

> With great affection, the Holy Father entrusts you to the protection and care of Mary, Health of the Sick. As a pledge of grace and peace in Christ our Savior, he cordially imparts to you and your family his Apostolic Blessing.[3]

On Gene's picture were written the words,[4]

> *Cum benedictione*
> Johannes Paulus II
> 5.1.97

That day was the feast of St. John Neumann. Frank Bassett recalls that evening:

> We talked about the seminary. He was always so concerned about our class. He told me that he

didn't think that he would make it to ordination in 2000. That was one thing that he wanted more than anything else. He had said . . . as a priest, he would be able to say Mass at the High Altar in Heaven with the High Priest, Jesus Christ. But if it were God's will that he be ordained and that it was early and simplex ordination, that would be fine also. *Fiat Voluntas Tua*. This would mean that at least he would be able to say Mass for his family and friends. We got back to Dunwoodie and talked for a long time.[5]

This was the first time that Gene had been in class for a month. He was just holding on. After his death his tenacity would cause Cardinal O'Connor to observe that Gene refused to leave the seminary on his own accord, because he wanted so much to be a priest.[6]

Gentle Goodbyes

During the next few days, while at Dunwoodie, Gene made it a point to visit various priests who had been important to him. These were, in fact, for the most part the last meetings. He went to see Father Thomas Derivan, his spiritual director, at St. Helena's Rectory. He also visited Monsignor James Sullivan at St. Eugene's Rectory. They spoke for an hour-and-a-half.

In the midst of all this, the husband of the telephone receptionist at Dunwoodie, Mary Sortino, had died. Mary's husband Peter had been ill for a long time with cancer. Gene insisted on going to the wake and spoke for some time with Mary and her daughter. They were well aware that he was himself dying. During this time also at the seminary, Gene had conversations with Bishop O'Brien, Monsignor Farley, and other priests there who had been very important in his life. He also called me on the sixteenth and we had a short conversation about the book that I was writing, which he thought was to be on the priesthood. He mentioned that he had started a book, too, and he wanted me to know about it. His voice was hoarse. I did not tell him that the book I was working on was about him and the priesthood.

During that period at Dunwoodie, Gene had to miss class rather frequently, and on Friday the seventeenth returned to the hospital. He was having very bad fits of coughing and began to appear agitated. This agitation is caused primarily by anoxia, or the inability of the lungs to introduce enough oxygen into the blood stream. A very similar experience is recorded in the diary of St. Thérèse of Lisieux when she was dying of tuberculosis. She also became quite agitated and was plunged into a period of great darkness. On January 20, Frank had gone to the hospital to visit Gene. As soon as he got the chance he took his oxygen mask off with a big smile and said, "How's everything at the seminary?"[7] He was wondering how this student and that were doing.

We now return to Margaret's account of the events of January 1997:

> The next day, January 12, Gene left for Dunwoodie. It was decided that the same few people would be updated. The first was Bishop O'Brien. Gene worried about telling him. Gene didn't want to hurt him or upset him. On Wednesday, Gene was beeped by Dr. Bhardwaj's office. The doctor had decided on a treatment plan and wanted him in his office on Thursday and in the hospital to start treatment on Friday.
>
> Gene Sr. picked up Gene at Dunwoodie and we all met at Good Samaritan Hospital. For the first time, I noticed that Gene Jr. was anxious. . . . The next morning Tom, Gene, and I left for Good Samaritan. All went well at admitting. Tom stayed

with him. Treatment started. That evening Gene was his usual cheerful self.

When I arrived at the hospital on Saturday, January 18 at 11:45 a.m., I breezed into the room, kissed Gene, and asked him how he was. "Not too good," was his reply. Then he started to cough. He coughed for over an hour straight and couldn't get his breath. Twice, he vomited some blood. Dr. Bhardwaj was called, Gene was given morphine to calm him down. Blood gases were taken and an oxygen mask was placed on his face. Gene Sr. and Tom came shortly later. The doctor discussed an in-hospital DNR [Do-Not-Resuscitate] order with Gene (and us). Gene signed one. Dr. Bhardwaj discussed Gene's condition with Gene Sr. and me in the hall. X rays revealed that Gene's right lung was "shot" from chemo, radiation, and pneumonia. If put on a respirator, he probably would not be able to get off it. Dr. Bhardwaj also felt that Gene would get over this episode. Death did not appear to be imminent. However, chemo treatment for the day was discontinued. I wanted to stay with Gene that night, but Gene urged me to go home, saying that he would need me more when he got home.

Sunday was a much calmer day. I arrived at 10:00 a.m. Monsignor Farley came shortly afterwards and celebrated Mass in the room. While Monsignor Farley was there, Dr. Bhardwaj came in to see Gene. He gave Gene the option of discontinuing treatment or slowing down the current treatment. Gene was adamant. "I want you to continue," he said. For most of the day, I sat and held Gene's hand. I prayed the Rosary aloud. Monday was very similar to Sunday. Treatment continued. Gene kept saying that he wanted to come home. We decided that Gene Sr. would take off on Tuesday. I would take off on Wednesday, the twenty-second. Before I left, I happened to turn up the volume on the Chapel Channel. The song *"Tu es sacerdos"* ["You are a Priest"] was playing. I was furious at myself, especially when I saw Gene's eyes. They were so sad. He remarked that he wanted to come home, regain his strength, and get back to Dunwoodie.[8]

You Are to Be a Priest

For months Gene had been telling very close friends quietly and peacefully that he somehow knew he would be a priest. At times he wondered whether he was right about this himself, but there was this intuition, this conviction quietly held that somehow he would be a priest. This was about to happen. Margaret tells the story:

> That night [January 20] around 9:30 Gene Sr. and I received a phone call from Bishop O'Brien that put everything in a new light. He told us that Cardinal O'Connor had called him to tell him that a fax had come that day from Rome. The Pope had granted the necessary dispensations. Gene was going to be ordained. We could hardly believe it. We were so happy for Gene.
>
> The next morning we met Bishop O'Brien shortly before 7:00 a.m. in the lobby of Good Samaritan. Together we went to Gene's room where the bishop gave Gene the call to orders. Gene quietly accepted the call, almost too overcome to realize that his dream was coming true. I saw a happiness in his eyes. I left to go to school.
>
> The reaction of people was one of jubilation.

The school children in St. Peter's cheered and clapped. One fourth grader yelled out a resounding "Yes." Later, when I told Gene, he was really moved. He said, "They did!" Many upon hearing the news then realized just how sick Gene was. All were happy that Gene's dream would be fulfilled.[9]

The fax received from Cardinal Pio Laghi is such a key part of this remarkable event that we take the liberty of reprinting it here. This letter explicitly mentions the possibility of a cure since it provides for what is to be done if this occurs. The dispensation itself also provided permission to omit the usual interval of time between the ordination to the diaconate and the priesthood:

Rome, 17 January 1997

Your Eminence,

This Congregation has received by fax your letter of 11 January last concerning the possibility of an early ordination for Mr. Eugene Richard Hamilton.

Given the peculiarities of the case we are disposed, with the approval of the Holy Father, to grant the necessary dispensation from studies required for ordination. In fact, when informed of the case, the Holy Father wished that his blessing, *toto corde*, be passed on to Mr. Hamilton.

This dispensation is given taking into account Bishop O'Brien's assurances that were Mr. Hamilton to be blessed with a cure of his illness, he would complete the normal seminary course of studies. Please find the dispensation enclosed. We are sending this by fax. The originals will follow in the diplomatic bag to the Apostolic Pro-Nuncio.

Please assure Mr. Hamilton of our prayers and
best wishes for him at this time.

Assuring Your Eminence of our most cordial
best wishes, we remain

Sincerely Yours in Christ,
Pio Card. Laghi

In the midst of all this startling good news, it was possible
to lose sight of the seriousness of the situation for a few minutes. These were days of incredible light and darkness. As Gene
left the hospital on that day, he signed an out-of-hospital do-
not-resuscitate order. He was well aware of the seriousness of
his condition after talking to the doctor and expressed his concern about his parents and Tom. Gene returned home using
oxygen and tried to use as little of it as he could, hoping that he
could get back to Dunwoodie.

That afternoon I, among several others, called Gene to tell
him we rejoiced with him and prayed for him. I happened at
that time to be at EWTN in Birmingham, Alabama. It struck
me when I spoke to Gene on the phone that he was quite short
of breath. He was very gentle and calm about the news of his
coming ordination. He quietly reminded me that this news
meant he was certainly going to die. We had all been praying
for one of two miracles: either that he would recover and become a priest, or that he would receive a dispensation for ordination before his death. Like many others, I was deeply moved
and immediately knelt before the exposed Blessed Sacrament
in the chapel of the Poor Clare Convent at the Eternal Word
Center in Birmingham.

Thursday, January 23, was a mysterious day. Naturally everyone was talking about the ordination; the diaconate was
to be the following Monday, and ordination to the priesthood
on the Saturday after that. Obviously everyone needed to talk,
to make some plans. Frank Bassett was sent to a religious
tailor to get an alb for the diaconate. But people noticed that

Gene himself was not participating in this excitement. He was on very heavy medication, which the doctor informed the family caused both stress and anxiety. His parents were coming out of the room as Gene and Frank Bassett sat together. Finally, when everyone left the room Gene talked about friendship — what it meant to him. Frank writes, "It sounded like a finality in the way he talked. I was getting a little scared because I sensed that the ordination was going to take a toll on him."[10]

When asked how he was, Gene said he was okay and just apprehensive. He wanted Frank to assure him that if they put him in the hospital again Frank would get him out. He began to be very weak. That afternoon it was decided that the diaconate would not be given at Dunwoodie, but would be given at home with his classmates present.

Friday, January 24 — Day of Sorrow, Day of Victory

Margaret writes in her diary that Friday, January 24, began normally — as normally as possible, that is. Even though Gene was uneasy with oxygen, he was able to accompany his mother at Morning Prayer, Rosary, and the prayer for the cause of Cardinal Cooke. Tom had arrived home from school the previous evening. Gene had greeted him warmly. "I'm so glad you're home. You're here to take care of me." Tom recalls that there was "the sound of desperation in his voice."[11] Although his father and mother for the most part were unaware of it, Gene hardly slept at all that night.

During conversations in the night, when Tom rubbed his brother's shoulders to relieve the pain and anxiety, Gene confessed that it was a relief now that everyone knew how sick he was because he was being ordained early. He did not have to hide his condition any more. This seems to be the first indication that Gene found it a struggle to always put on a smiling face.

That night will be etched in Tom's memory for the rest of his life. He writes:

At around 2:00 a.m., while we were sitting on the couch, Gene told me how happy he was to have me for a brother and Frank Bassett for a best friend. He thanked me and told me how much he loved me. I attributed this to his anxiety and so I tried to calm him down. During the night, I think he asked me to say the Chaplet of Divine Mercy out loud so that he could hear it and he would pray along with it.

At around 4:00 a.m., Gene again started talking to me. This time he was talking about death. He stated that many people died because they didn't have the oxygen machine that he had and that he really shouldn't be alive. Since he had just awoke from a brief sleep, I simply attributed this to a bad dream, of which he had many, as well as anxiety. I told him not to worry because he was going to live because he had the oxygen machine.[12]

Tom often mentions that Gene was anxious these last hours of his life. It should be observed that a serious shortness of breath and lack of oxygen in the system bring on a powerful reaction that can quickly become panic. You know this if you have ever for any reason been unable to breathe for a period of time. Breathing is the most urgent and imperative physical need we can experience. This anxiety on the part of Gene should not be seen as a retreat from his long endeavor to accept God's will in all things. St. Thérèse of Lisieux, who was a person totally surrendered to God's will and Providence, suffered such anxiety in the last days of her life when she also experienced shortness of breath and the lack of oxygen.[13] Actually, if one reads the testimony of Mother Agnes, the sister of St. Thérèse, there are several parallels between the death of this saint and of Eugene Hamilton.

Margaret and Gene Sr. went to work thinking that their son

was going to have a normal day, considering his illness. With Tom home, he was in good hands. As the morning went on, the two brothers again recited the Divine Mercy Chaplet, and Gene asked Tom to repeat over and over, "My Jesus, mercy." He told Tom that this was the only thing that helped him control his anxiety. Frank Bassett called, and then they watched the daily Mass from St. Patrick's Cathedral.

For the next several hours Tom is our only witness. Like the diary of his mother, his testimony is well-written and has a ring of reality that no narration of a third person can give:

> Between 11:00 a.m. and 1:00 p.m., Gene ate eggs and soup. He was very hungry. He asked me to call a few of his friends to tell them when his ordination would be the next week. After I got off the phone, he would ask me, "Do they realize how serious this is?" I remember him telling me not to go upstairs and leave him alone downstairs. I think he was afraid he was going to die alone. I didn't realize it at the time. In addition to the outgoing phone calls, Gene received three incoming calls — Father Thomas Derivan, his spiritual director; Monsignor Farley, spiritual director of the seminary; and Father Benedict Groeschel, the promoter of Cardinal Cooke's cause. It struck me that the three priests who had the most direct impact on his spiritual life called almost one after the other. I remember him speaking to one of the priests about his ordination. Immediately, with seemingly no reason, he said, "Father, please pray that I go gently" (I think he was talking to Monsignor Farley). I was surprised that he went from talking about his ordination to asking the priest to pray that he die gently.
>
> At around 1:00 p.m., Father Benedict called to

talk to Gene. Gene was now having a very hard time breathing and he gave the phone to me to talk to Father. Father Benedict asked me to get a tape recorder and have Gene tape record his feelings about being ordained a priest over the next week.[14]

At the end of this conversation about taping, I spoke to him for a minute or two. He was breathless and anxious. I had placed this phone call from a retreat house in California. Although I had definitely decided not to call, not to trouble Gene, not to waste money, I was persistently troubled by the thought that I should call.

After I spoke to Gene I regretted that I had ever mentioned the tape recorder. I got Tom on the phone and told him I thought Gene was dying, and to call his parents and tell them to come home immediately. I had been the infirmarian for years in the seminary and I had attended the dying several times. I also called the seminary and alerted Father Joseph Tierney, the procurator, to contact Bishop O'Brien and make him aware of the situation. Naturally I was praying at the retreat and was hoping that I was wrong.

Father Kelly came for a visit. He mentioned to Tom, "I hate to see him in so much pain."[15] Tom continues:

Between 2:00 p.m. and 3:00 p.m., Gene started to become more anxious. At the same time, however, I remember, he became quiet. And then he said to me, and these are the last words that I remember him saying, "All I want to do is God's Will in my life. And I'm only afraid I'm not going to be able to do what He wants of me." He seemed very upset. I thought he was going to cry because he was so upset that he wasn't going to be able to fulfill what God wanted him to do. He wasn't looking at me when he said this. Gene and I rarely ever talked about his spiritual life. He had a deep faith, a great sense of humility, and a very deep spirituality. I knew this and never asked him any questions. So, I didn't understand why he was saying this for apparently no reason. These were the last words that I remember him saying.

At about 3:00 p.m., my Mom arrived home. When she went in to see him, she asked him how he was doing. He told her he wasn't feeling well. Then I went into the room and realized that he was "zoning out." His eyes weren't focusing and his body started to lean forward. My Mom came into the room and held him up in the recliner he was sitting in saying, "Gene, I love you," over and over again. We thought he was having an allergic reaction to medication. At the same time, the home health-care nurse from Good Samaritan Hospital came in and tried to take Gene's blood pressure and heart beat while my Mom held him in her arms. After calling the paramedics, I called Father Kelly our pastor and told him Gene was dying. The paramedics arrived and placed Gene on the floor. Father Kelly came back and knelt beside Gene on the floor and administered the Anointing of the Sick. My father was called next and told to go to Good Samaritan Hospital, but then we told him to come home, not to the hospital. I called Bishop O'Brien and told him Gene was dying and asked him to come to Haverstraw. Frank Bassett, Gene's friend, called and I told him Gene was dying. Frank told me he would come right up. The paramedics placed Gene on the couch. After anointing him, Father Kelly knelt by his head thanking him for teaching him so much about the priesthood. My

Mom and I also stayed with him and we told him not to be afraid to die. This is what he told our Aunt Ann MacDonald the night before she died of cancer.[16]

You Are a Priest

The minutes were ticking away as earthly life was fading. All the plans, the letter to the Holy Father, the dispensation, the hopes for the priesthood were about to disappear with the mysterious onset of death. The physical and the spiritual were locked in combat and it looked this time like the physical was going to prevail. But Tom continues:

> At around 4:00 p.m., the side door swung open as Bishop O'Brien ran through the doorway with a stole, holy oils, and a "Rites" book under his arm. He walked up to the couch, bent over, and said, "Eugene, we're going to make you a priest!" He put the stole over his head, opened the rites book, administered the laying on of hands, and said prayers for his ordination to the diaconate. Laying his hands on him, Bishop O'Brien said, "Gene, you are now a deacon and soon you will be a priest!" He turned a few pages and again began the rite of ordination, this time for the priesthood. He administered the laying on of hands and then anointed Gene's hands with chrism. Then he congratulated Father Gene on being a priest. Bishop O'Brien and my mother placed the stole around Gene's shoulders. I remember the bishop commenting that Gene had certainly earned his ordination and was very worthy to be a priest.[17]

Bishop O'Brien recalls that after the ordination all recited the *Salve Regina*, the favorite prayer of Cardinal Cooke. How deeply meaningful the words of this prayer must have sounded that winter afternoon in the Hamilton living room — "mourning and weeping in this valley of tears. Turn then, Most Gracious Advocate, thine eyes of mercy towards us, and after this our exile, show unto us the blessed fruit of thy womb, Jesus." The completely providential aspect of this ordination should be lost on no one. With the exception of Cardinal O'Connor himself, few bishops would have taken the responsibility of ordaining a dying man. There would be questions and there would be critics.

Bishop O'Brien, on the other hand, knew the whole story better than anyone else. He commented later to me that the words of the Holy Father, *"Toto corde"* — From my whole heart — were running through his mind as he drove to Haverstraw in the rain. After the ordination the bishop immediately called Cardinal O'Connor, who also saw the providential aspects of this remarkable event. He was most reassuring to Bishop O'Brien and was deeply moved to prayer by what had happened. Later, after Father Gene's death, the Bishop would again call the cardinal, who then spoke to Margaret — words of condolence and also of congratulations. Faith will tell you why it was to be. The hour had come. Faith is. It is more than an act of intellect and will. Faith is far more than even the most profound words in which its dogmas are enshrined. It is even more than the translated human words containing direct divine revelation. Faith in Christ as Son of God means that we know that He is present. That He was present in the living room of the house in Haverstraw anyone with faith ought to be able to acknowledge.

The Paschal Mystery

Gene was a priest and now he was to be united with the Paschal Mystery of Christ, the King who was crowned with thorns and enthroned on a Cross while the mob shouted "Crucify him" rather than "Long live the King." Christ is the only King who ever died at His own coronation, because His Kingdom was not of this world. His young and fervent disciple, so improbably a priest, was about to follow him. He was to die at his own ordination. We have two other accounts of this last hour of Gene's life written by Bishop O'Brien and Frank Bassett. Rather than trying to collate these and lose their individual emphases, I have decided to use Frank's and Tom's now and then to use Bishop O'Brien's memories as part of Gene's funeral sermon, when he shared them with all. Frank Bassett was rushing through the rain saying the Rosary. He arrived at the house not knowing if the ordination had taken place:

> As Tom opens the door of the house, he tells me that Gene had just been ordained a priest by the Bishop. I am so happy. Tom tells me to come to the den. I go in. Mrs. Hamilton, Bishop O'Brien, Father Charles Kelly, and Tom and I are in the room. Gene is lying on the couch. His breathing is very labored. He is on oxygen and at times he is agitated. But he seems peaceful. The Bishop is continuing with prayers, litanies, and prayers of commendation for Gene. Father Kelly goes to the end of the couch where Gene's head is and he kneels down and holds Gene's shoulders. Mrs. Hamilton is on a chair near Gene's left side and is stroking his arm. She is telling him to calm down. Tom is at the opposite end of the couch as Father Kelly and is telling Gene he is a priest. Father Gene! I also notice that Gene seems to be jaundiced and pale. The only thing I can think of is that his liver has shut down. I feel that all the treatments have finally taken their toll. He is actively dying. His eyes are partially open but he does not speak because he is so weak. He is told that his Dad is coming, to hold on. Tom then tells Gene that I am there. I say, "Congratulations, Father

Gene," and sit on the couch edge near the end where Tom is touching Gene's legs. I take his left hand into mine. He has the Rosary which the Pope sent him in his hand. His fingers are touching my palm and he begins to tap into my palm. It is not an unconscious reaction. He is tapping deliberately to tell me that he knows that I am there. He also attempts to make, what I believe is, a Sign of the Cross in my palm. I remember the conversation we had the day before that I only wanted a first blessing from him. I feel overwhelmed and blessed. With all that is happening to him, he still wants to give me something from him.

Bishop O'Brien asked me to call the seminary and tell them that Gene was ordained a priest. I call Father Tierney and tell him to tell the community and ask that they pray for Gene because it is really bad. He says okay. I go back to the room and Bishop O'Brien begins a Rosary. Gene is still agitated. He is told that his Dad is on his way. His Mom keeps telling him to say "Jesus." Gene seems to be attempting to say "Jesus" but he is so weak. We see his teeth moving trying to say the word "Jesus." I think that they had talked about this before. The Bishop finishes the Rosary and calls the Cardinal to tell him that Gene is dying and he had to ordain him a deacon and priest. The Cardinal talks to Mrs. Hamilton. Tom, Father Kelly, and I stay with Gene. Mrs. Hamilton and the Bishop come back into the room. Father Kelly is telling Gene that he was so great. He taught Father Kelly so much. He is a priest. He also says that he did so much for so many people. He says he's a great kid.

. . . The visiting nurse, Judy, arrives. She looks

in on Gene and sees us all praying there with him. The Bishop is still leading us in prayer. Dr. Bhardwaj arrives around 5:30 or 6. . . . I am saying "Father Gene" and rubbing his shoulders. His father takes the piece of Cardinal Cooke's cassock and places it on Gene's chest. . . . We are all calling him Father Gene. His mother is telling him to get ready to go to Jesus. His breathing is about the same. Very labored. Dr. Bhardwaj comes in and listens to Gene's lungs. He says that his lungs are clear and that his heart is strong. We continue to stay with Gene. Mrs. Hamilton and the nurse leave the room with the doctor. Father Kelly begins to say some prayers. Deacon Hamilton then says a Rosary and we all participate. Deacon Hamilton and Mrs. Hamilton are now sitting in chairs at the edge of the couch. The Bishop is standing. Tom is at the end of the couch near Gene's feet. The Bishop and Mrs. Hamilton had put the Bishop's stole on Gene earlier, before Deacon Hamilton arrived. At one point Gene said, "I have to go," or "I'm going now!" At another point while Tom, his Dad, and I were in the room with me behind Gene's head, Tom told me that he sees tears coming from Gene's eyes.[18]

During all this drama, Tom is the one who is the most calm. His best friend and brother is dying, but he has to keep things together. He does not take time out to think of himself, but of all the others beginning with his parents. He has learned the lesson well from his big brother to put himself last. Frank Bassett comments on Tom:

Tom's composure and sense of mind was extraordinary and was the reason why Gene's dream of priesthood was fulfilled before he died. If it had not been for Tom this would not have happened.[19]

His Suffering is Over

Tom himself continues describing the events:

> At 5:00 p.m., my father arrived home and . . . held Gene's hand and didn't say anything. He didn't have to! Gene knew he was there. At one point, Gene said to my mother, "I'm going away now." My mother kept telling him that we would all be okay and he could go to Jesus. My mother kept repeating, "Jesus, Jesus, Jesus!" Gene also mouthed the Name of Jesus over and over again. While no sound came from his mouth, I saw his tongue move against his teeth and he mouthed "Jesus" with my mother. During the last hour, I saw one or two tears roll down his face. They didn't seem to be tears of pain or suffering. His anxiety and fear ended when my father came. He knew he was ordained a priest forever! The tears rolled down his cheeks as he was getting closer to death. During the last half hour before his death, Gene's breathing slowed. His breaths became shorter and shorter. At 7:04 p.m., Father Gene Hamilton was the most peaceful he has ever been in many years. It was a relief to see that his suffering was finally over.[20]

Jesus was Lying There

Frank Bassett now recalls the very last minutes of Gene's earthly life:

> Finally around 6:55 we are all in the room. Gene's breathing becomes more labored. We con-

tinue to pray. Then Gene's breathing becomes very sporadic and slow. He finally stops breathing at 7:04. Father Kelly and I kneel down after making a Sign of the Cross. Dr. Bhardwaj makes the Sign of the Cross also when we did. I remember Gene telling me that Dr. Bhardwaj had gone to Catholic school and that he was teaching him, a Hindu, how to make the Sign of the Cross. He was always constantly trying to evangelize for God. That's Gene! It is now peaceful. Gene is with God. Father Kelly, Judy the visiting nurse, Dr. Bhardwaj, the Bishop, and I leave the room. Tom, Deacon, and Mrs. Hamilton say good-bye to Gene. They come out. Dr. Bhardwaj says how he thought that he saw Jesus lying there. Tom and I go back into the room. The Bishop calls the Seminary and tells them that Gene died. The nurse and Dr. Bhardwaj had left. Tom and I just comfort each other with the fact that Gene is Father Gene. He is a priest forever. We say that he looks the most peaceful than he had in one-and-a-half years. The picture of Gene signed by the Pope is in a frame on a table behind him. . . .

I think, "It has been a long fight and you won, Gene. You are a priest. We will miss you but you are with your Lord. The sacrifice of the Mass was not celebrated in the way we know but Gene was the sacrifice this night. What more can someone do than give himself to God?" Father Kelly, the Hamiltons and I sit and talk for a long while. I leave and return to the Seminary.[21]

Endnotes

1. Diary of Margaret Hamilton, 21-23.
2. Ibid., 23-24.

3. Letter of January 10, 1997, from Monsignor L. Sandri, Assessor, on behalf of Pope John Paul II.

4. Diary, insert for 24.

5. Frank Bassett, Memoir of Father Eugene R. Hamilton, 2-3.

6. John Cardinal O'Connor, "This Is the Church" (Homily of February 2, 1997), Catholic New York, February 6, 1997: 15.

7. Bassett, Memoir, 7.

8. Diary, 24-26.

9. Ibid., 26-27.

10. Bassett, Memoir, 9.

11. Statement of Thomas Hamilton, 1.

12. Ibid., 2.

13. Guy Gaucher, *The Passion of Thérèse of Lisieux*: 4 April — 30 September 1897 (New York: Crossroad, 1990), 90-95.

14. T. Hamilton, Statement, 3-4.

15. Ibid., 4.

16. Ibid., 4-5.

17. Ibid., 5-6.

18. Bassett, Memoir, 11-13.

19. Ibid., 10.

20. T. Hamilton, Statement, 6-7.

21. Bassett, Memoir, 13-14.

10

There Is Sorrow — There Is Joy

Rev. Eugene Hamilton, Jr. **Dedication** 1972 - 1997

"From the day of his ordination, a priest can never forget that he has been called by God Himself. The Priest is called to be a Servant...a Victim...a Brother...a Listener...a Friend... The anointing that Jesus gives us is to help us bring His into our world..."

Terence Cardinal Cooke

"There is sorrow that he will never preach a homily. But there is joy that his life has taught us more than he could ever say." These words are taken from a poem written by Deacon Hamilton the day after his son's funeral. The days between Friday evening, January 24, and the funeral on Wednesday, January 29, were days of incredible heights and depths of feeling for the Hamiltons, and for hundreds of others: from Cardinal O'Connor and the clergy and seminarians to the citizens of Rockland County who read about the young man who died at his ordination. Surely among the great crowds of the City, many read with sympathy Charles Bell's article in the *Daily News*, "Born To Be and Died a Priest".[1]

Throughout all of this Margaret, Gene Sr., and Tom did exactly what Father Gene would have done. They were there for everybody else — and there were many. Most of the people who participated in any part of the funeral were so deeply moved that they felt strongly that they had to say something to the Hamiltons. And although like most families at such a time, the Hamiltons wanted to be quiet with their own thoughts, they fulfilled this responsibility as members of the community of faith, of the Mystical Body of Christ. They were there to greet, to listen, to thank people for coming to join them in prayer. If you were not present (and I was away giving a retreat on the West Coast) you have the challenge of putting together in your mind the sorrow of a funeral of a very young man with the joy of a first Mass. It is a tribute to all involved that they were able to put these two painfully different events together. Having listened to many who were present, I realize that those few days in January are almost impossible to describe.

Fortunately, the Saturday and Sunday before the funeral were given to the Hamiltons as days of preparation, and a little bit of silence. On Monday afternoon, dressed for the first time in the vestments of a priest, the body of Father Eugene Hamilton was placed before the high altar in the chapel of St. Joseph's Seminary. Over fifty priests concelebrated with Bishop O'Brien the Mass of the Holy Eucharist that evening. Many transitional and permanent deacons assisted at the Mass as well. We have seen that Bishop O'Brien was there for Gene from the very first days of his illness to his ordination. His homily at the Mass that evening gives us an opportunity to appreciate the Bishop's feelings as an essential figure in this drama.

A Priest — "Someone I Become"

First Bishop O'Brien described his feelings of love and appreciation for the Church that was so responsive to an individual's concern. He then told of his joy at telling Gene's parents the good news in the evening that their son was to be ordained. Together with them he awakened Gene at the hospital on Tuesday morning with the ecstatic news of the dispensation. The Bishop told of their plans for a formal ordination, which had to be bypassed, and then he described the ordination as he remembered it:

> Within twenty-four hours of that agreement, a little past three o'clock Friday afternoon, Tom Hamilton — so noble throughout — telephoned to ask that I come to their home quickly, that Gene had taken a bad turn. Tom, his mother, Margaret, and their pastor, Father Charles Kelly, surrounded Gene with prayer. So labored was his breathing that I thought it prudent to proceed with the essential forms of the ordinations: opening prayer, laying on of hands and the ordination prayer, first for diaconate, then for priesthood, followed by the anointing of hands with chrism. Thereafter, his father Deacon Eugene (having arrived home from work in New York) helped Margaret and me place my stole over their new priest's head and around his shoulders.
>
> As I spoke my intention and prayed the ordination rite in loud, clear tones for Gene to hear, thoughts of Samuel came alive as at last he hears the whisper of the Lord's call in his sleep. Periodic efforts on Gene's part to speak (and he did say quite distinctly at one point, "I have to leave") led me to suspect that he was aware of what was happening, aware that the priesthood he so desperately desired with his whole being was now close at hand. Not that he had ever asked for or even hinted at a dispensation for an early ordination, surely. But he

never, ever surrendered his deep trust in the Providence of God that somehow, all this would work out to a blessed solution. What to the rest of us seemed like irreconcilable, even deadly foes — a distant priesthood and an all-consuming, rapacious, galloping cancer — Gene was convinced would find a resolution he could live with. A resolution there was, and live with it he will — for all eternity. Yes, he was open to the reception of Holy Orders with his whole being, and how generous the Lord was in fulfilling that desire. But not without the intervention of the Vicar of Christ on earth in Rome, the Cardinal Archbishop of New York, and a rookie bishop who still finds it difficult to believe that his "Here I am, Lord" would involve him in such miracles of Providence.[2]

Bishop O'Brien then spoke of the theology of the priesthood, a theology under attack as we shall discuss in the Addendum. He reminded the congregation that the "priesthood is not something I do, primarily; it is something I am, or better still, Someone I become."[3]

The Bishop then cited two important passages from the *Catechism of the Catholic Church* on the priesthood: "Through that sacrament [ordination] priests by the anointing of the Holy Spirit are signed with a special character and so are configured to Christ the priest in such a way that they are able to act in the person of Christ the head" (CCC 1563).[4]

"Through the ordained ministry, especially that of bishops and priests, the presence of Christ as head of the Church is made visible in the midst of the community of believers" (CCC 1549).[5]

The Bishop then continued:

"The presence of Christ made visible. . . ." And as we privileged few gathered about that only priestly altar Gene would know to be his own in this earthly existence, the sofa on which he lay prostrate and face-up during his ordination, as he offered his priestly sacrifice to God, what kind of visible presence of Christ did Father Eugene Hamilton herald?

Our Church tells us that all who suffer, and in a unique way her priests, contribute in an eminent way to the work of redemption. Pope John Paul II, himself no stranger to the sick-bed altar of sacrifice, says that those rendered helpless by illness "continue to be active members for the building up of the Church, especially by virtue of their union with the suffering Christ and with so many other brothers and sisters in the Church who are sharing in the Lord's Passion" (Colossians 1:24). They relive, the Pope says, Paul's spiritual experience when he said, "I rejoice in my sufferings for your sake, and in my flesh I complete what is lacking in Christ's afflictions for the sake of his body, that is, the Church"(*Pastores Dabo Vobia* 77).[6]

A First Mass

Bishop O'Brien, after giving a brief history of Gene's illness and ordination, described how he had afterwards supplied the non-essential prayers and readings. He then said what all present felt — that this Mass was in fact Father Gene's First Mass. He concluded his sermon by asking the congregation to supply the other part of the ceremony that had yet to be done — namely, the sign of the congregation's assent and approval. One seminarian described this to me later saying that you could feel the descent of the Holy Spirit in the electrified atmosphere of the chapel as the whole congregation signaled its approval.

Toward the end of the Mass, Deacon Hamilton expressed the gratitude of the family to so many people involved, beginning with the Holy Father. He then read a letter of Father Gene's telling of his devotion to the Servant of God Cardinal Cooke and his reliance on the prayer of the Cardinal that he would be a priest of the Archdiocese.[7]

"United with the Suffering of Christ"

Father Gene's body was then taken to his home parish of St. Peter in Haverstraw, the only parish he had ever known. His body lay in state in the church until Wednesday morning, when his funeral Mass was offered by John Cardinal O'Connor. The Cardinal recalled that he had encouraged Eugene and the other servers to think of the priesthood at the Mass offered for the repose of the soul of Father Pastor Rafer in that church ten years before. Cardinal O'Connor, who as we have seen had been in frequent contact with Gene during his illness and who had personally sent the petition for his ordination to Cardinal Pio Laghi, often spoke of Gene in homilies and talks in the week ahead. On the following Sunday, February 2, in his sermon at St. Patrick's Cathedral, the Cardinal said:

> This man absolutely refused to leave the seminary except to go to the hospital to be treated for the devastating cancer. . . .
> . . . But all his life he burned with a desire to be a priest. During this long period of his almost unbelievable suffering he came more and more to unite that suffering with the suffering of Christ on the Cross and to offer it for you and for me.[8]

The Cardinal also used this opportunity to counter those who are constantly criticizing the Church. He said:

> For those who see nothing but a big, grim, monstrous, bureaucratic, institutional Church, let

it be known that not only did our Holy Father grant the dispensation immediately, but he said, "Give Eugene all of my love. Tell him I love him with my whole heart." He used the Latin phrase *"in toto corde."*[9]

"Never More Powerful"

The sermon at the funeral Mass, attended by over eight hundred people, was given by Father Gene's spiritual director, Father Thomas Derivan. Again, the preacher linked the life and death of Father Gene to the experience of Cardinal Cooke, to whom he was so closely united. Father Derivan quoted from words that Gene had written three years before: "The greatest manifestation of the love of Christ was seen when He spread His arms on the Cross. Thus the priest must take up his Cross like Christ and must suffer like Christ." Father Derivan continued:

> Those words were prophetic. Priesthood and the Cross were mystically joined in this priest. He was ordained a priest not in the glory of a cathedral, but in the holiness of a sickbed. As you know he had great devotion to our late revered Cardinal Cooke, faithful Servant of God. He learned from Cardinal Cooke the sanctity of life even when weakened, even when the earthen vessel seemed so fragile. But just as His Eminence has said of Cardinal Cooke that he was never more powerful than when he suffered, so too Father Hamilton was never more what he was meant to be than in his fragile weakness. He was strong in faith, strong in love for you, for the Church, for the priesthood. He was a priest for a day; now he is priest for eternity.[10]

Again, Deacon Hamilton thanked everyone and reminded the parishioners of his son's love and devoted service to the parish. Margaret then spoke in Spanish to the Hispanic community and reminded them that Father Gene had been working on being fluent in Spanish. She told of how Father Gene was so delighted at the enthusiastic applause of the school children when they heard that he was to be ordained. There was also here an opportunity to thank Dr. Bhardwaj and the staff of Good Samaritan Hospital and all the medical personnel who had been such faithful friends. Deacon Hamilton ended with a recitation of the quotation from Cardinal Cooke that appeared on Gene's ordination card.

"Gift and Mystery"

Then recalling the title of the Pope's own book on the occasion of his fiftieth anniversary to the priesthood, *Gift and Mystery*, he gave the following farewell which deeply moved all in the church:

> Although today we are proud parents, we cannot even try to sing our son's many praises. Perhaps the words which best describe him are that "he was a son any parent would be proud to have had."
>
> Margaret and I believe that we have been witnesses to an extraordinary intervention of God's grace in our son's life! And we stand here today with Mary, the Mother of Jesus, at the foot of his Cross with broken hearts. But with hearts nevertheless filled with gratitude to Almighty God for the "Gift and Mystery" of our son's priesthood.[11]

The burial of Father Eugene took place immediately after the funeral Mass in the little plot for priests in St. Peter's Cemetery in Haverstraw. It is a quaint, rural kind of cemetery where some of the pioneers of the Catholic Church in Rockland County are interred, along with a small number of priests from recent years. Father Gene wished to be buried there with the priests and would have been, even if he had not been ordained. His selection of this site makes clear to those who understand the situation that despite his successes at college in New York City he was at heart always "a county boy." Values like home, parish, and familiar little towns were very much "in his blood." This is not said to disparage the sophisticated and more aggressive faith of city dwellers. I would hardly do that, but I simply wish to point out that Father Eugene Hamilton exemplified the very best human qualities of small-town America and that he could have been just as much at home in Nebraska or New Hampshire as he was in the beginnings of upstate New York. When I visited his grave at St. Peter's Cemetery amid the trees and old nineteenth-century-style headstones — and I knew that Gene had selected this spot — I realized for the first time that he was indeed a gentle sign of contradiction to the competitive, flashy mass culture which America appears to be irresistibly drawn to.

A Sign of Contradiction

Deacon Hamilton assessed his son's unique contribution in this way:

> We live in an age that has forgotten God and thinks it will live forever. We live in a society which rejects the idea of sin and believes it can do no wrong. We live in a Church where there are many who see no need for sacrifice or commitment. Some who go to church on Sunday see the priest only as a leader or spokesman of the assembly. They would like to replace him with a man or woman of their choice who will tell them what they want to hear. Amid all this downward spiral of life and faith, God has sent us another "sign of contradiction." He has sent us a priest who never

offered Mass, never absolved, never preached a homily, and who never blessed. Yet his life and death were a priestly sacrifice united to that one perfect sacrifice of Jesus. He was a priest in this most important essence. He was both victim and priest, as was Jesus. He is a sign of contradiction to what the modern world believes the priesthood will come to be.[12]

Touching Tributes

Even the memorials which an admiring community selects for those who stand out from their peers have in Gene's case a touchingly hometown quality. The Rockland County CYO will annually give a Father Eugene Hamilton Award to the member who shows the greatest leadership quality and concern for others as a young Christian. Moving down toward the city, but still retaining the very personal touch, the Campus Ministry Center at Manhattan College will be dedicated to Father Gene's memory and bear his name. And at St. Joseph's Seminary, which has always served as a bridge between the big city and the sprawling upper counties of the Archdiocese (an area one hundred eighty miles long), there will be a plaque on Gene's last choir stall in the chapel recalling his ordination and his first Mass.

Blessed are They That Walk in the Law of the Lord

Father Eugene Hamilton was such a fine and good man that it is possible to lose the greater significance of his life in the midst of his very admirable qualities. He lived long enough and wrote just enough to have a message which his own writings given in this book make clear. He was an ardent Christian in an age of unbelief. He was a man of sterling moral qualities in a time of public scandal and gross immorality. He was a devout and fervent Catholic who personally loved Christ, His Mother, the angels, and the saints at a time when many contemporary Christians are embarrassed by the personal piety which someone like Gene Hamilton so easily exhibited.

I consider it a defensible position to say that Eugene Hamilton would have been suspect and had a difficult time even surviving in a number of seminaries in the English-speaking world — simply because of his traditional piety and devotion. What Gene Hamilton believed in, stood for, and respected was not supposed to last; it was not supposed to be part of the "new church." And with all of this we do not find with Gene any strident statements, any breaking of the bruised reed, or quenching of the smoldering wick. When confronted with what he found deficient or even wrong, he quietly stood his ground and without much apparent struggle exhibited that charity which St. Paul describes so well in 1 Corinthians 13. He was "patient, kind, not provoked, inflated, or rude, but rejoicing at the truth." The Apostle says that "charity dares all things, believes all things, hopes all things, endures all things, and never fails." Could you find a better description for Eugene Hamilton?

It is a well-established fact in the study of spiritual development that after an individual achieves a life of moral integrity, firm faith, and total hope and trust in God, this person will enter into the illuminative way, a time of unbounded charity, love of neighbor, and then of God. These brief pages have described such a person. After these stages the great writers of the spiritual life describe what is ominously named the Dark Night of the Senses and of the Soul by St. John of the Cross. I believe that Gene did such a good job of coping with his fears and the darkness by genuine concern for all around him that he actually concealed some of his great struggles. We see them only partially revealed in his writings and behavior. In this way he very much imitated his chosen ideal in life, Terence Cardinal Cooke. We do see someone who is trying to make the best use out of every disappointing and catastrophic piece of medical information. We see someone who constantly tried by prayer and every other means to accept his terminal condition as a "grace-filled moment."[13] This phrase was taken from Cardinal Cooke, and Gene found it most enlightening.

Finally, as in the case of St. Thérèse of Lisieux (in whose centenary year Gene died), the bright light only came at the very end. Gene experienced the same elemental anxiety of St. Thérèse caused by the failure of the lungs and the loss of oxygen. God in His providence sent a bright beam of the transcendent light of eternity to Gene in the very last hours. With Thérèse it was only in the last minute. The ray of eternity was as it ought to be for someone called to be a priest: the sacramental gift of ordination — for others but also for himself. It is eminently true that the priesthood is given for all the members of the Church, but the individual priest himself is one of these members. He should not stoically be left out of the gift that is given to others through him.

When discussing all that had happened, I asked Bishop O'Brien if he had the impression that some of his actions were being directed by Providence in the last weeks of Gene's life. We learned that we had both felt the same way. We were not deprived of our freedom, but to put it simply, we were being nudged along. I asked others, and they also felt the same way. This was an unusual but common enough religious experience. It is so subtle that you must look back on it and ask yourself why you did this or that. The simple answer of faith is that we were supposed to. For those who do not believe, no explanation of this is possible; and for those who do believe no explanation is necessary. The Hour had come.

We might all learn from this gentle and remarkable young man that they are blessed who walk according to the Law of the Lord (Psalms 119:1), that for those who seek God all things work together unto good. The safest of all ways to live one's life is to put it into the hands of God and to say to the Father with Christ His Son "Thy Will be Done."

Endnotes

1. *Daily News*, February 8, 1997: 14.
2. Homily of Bishop Edwin F. O'Brien, Mass of the Holy Eucharist for Reverend Eugene Hamilton, January 27, 1997, 2-3.
3. Ibid., 3.
4. *Catechism of the Catholic Church*, English edition (*Libreria Editrice Vaticana*, 1994), 391.
5. Ibid., 387.
6. Homily of Bishop O'Brien, 3.
7. Deacon Eugene Hamilton, Sr., Eulogy for Father Eugene Hamilton, Jr., January 27, 1997.
8. John Cardinal O'Connor, "This Is the Church" (homily of February 2, 1997), *Catholic New York*, February 6, 1997: 15.
9. Ibid., 16.
10. Homily of Father Thomas Derivan, Funeral Mass for Father Eugene Hamilton, January 29, 1997.
11. Deacon Eugene Hamilton, Sr., Eulogy for Father Eugene Hamilton, Jr., January 29, 1997.
12. Diary of Deacon Eugene Hamilton, Sr., 1-2.
13. Terence Cardinal Cooke, *This Grace Filled Moment* (New York: The Rosemont Press, 1984). Available from Cardinal Cooke Guild, 1011 First Ave., New York, NY 10022.

Addendum I

Father Eugene R. Hamilton
Talk at End of Baccalaureate Mass, Manhattan College
Feast of Pentecost, May 22, 1994

As we cherish Christ's Real Presence within us, we are called to reflect about this feast of Pentecost, as well as the beginning of a new stage in our lives. In order to fully understand the role of the Holy Spirit among us and within the Church, we need to look at the first Pentecost, we need to look at the events on the Feast of Pentecost in the year 1694, and we need to look at Pentecost today.

That first Pentecost took place nine days after the Ascension of Our Lord. That nine days became the first novena, the first nine days of prayer that the Church offered to God for assistance and guidance. In the reading from the Acts of the Apostles for the feast of the Ascension, we are told of a baptism with the Holy Spirit that is to come. We are told by Christ Himself that "you are to be my witnesses . . . even to the ends of the earth." Last Sunday, the Seventh Sunday of Easter, we heard the prayer of Christ once again as He says to His Father, "As you have sent me into the world, so I have sent them into the world; I consecrate myself for their sakes now, that they may be consecrated in truth." And finally today, in the Gospel according to John, we see the followers of Christ gathered in the Upper Room, ready to be filled with the Passion that is the Paraclete, ready to be sent forth.

In 1694, there was another group of individuals gathered, ready in a sense to be filled with the Holy Spirit, ready to be sent forth. This group, gathered in France on the feast of Pentecost, was about to call upon this Gift of God, this Third Person of the Blessed Trinity, to help them establish a Rule and vows for their new religious order. The Brothers of the Christian Schools who were gathered that day with John Baptist De LaSalle sought to discern the Will of God in their individual lives but also for the life of their community. The Holy Spirit that was to move them would sustain the order up to this present day as one dedicated to teaching the poor and those less fortunate. The formula devised by De LaSalle and his Brothers has as its basic element consecration to the Triune God — the Father, the Son, and yes, the Holy Spirit. Interestingly enough, the major debate that Pentecost Sunday in 1694 centered upon the question of including the vow of chastity with their other vows of poverty and obedience.

Now exactly three hundred years later to the day, we are able to see how the Brothers eventually dealt with the question of the vow of chastity, recognizing its importance in living out the Christian life and specifically the religious life. Meanwhile we ourselves, on the brink of graduation, are called upon to exhibit the passion that is the Holy Spirit, the same Person of the Blessed Trinity to whom the Brothers consecrated themselves. By virtue of our Confirmation and our role as committed Catholics, we are obligated to give witness to Christ, as He commanded on the feast of the Ascension. By virtue of our role as individuals at a school with a LaSallian tradition, we are obligated to recognize the Spirit and the gifts given us by that same Spirit. By virtue of our role as the future leaders of the world and the Church, we are called upon to mirror the Love that exists between the Father and the Son; we are called upon to live out the Holy Spirit.

As the Class of 1994, that means having the wisdom, the knowledge, the fortitude, the piety, the fear of the Lord, the understanding, and the courage to be open to passion, and to be passionate. The Holy Spirit working through the Catholic Church, through Christ's Body, and through each of us, is waiting to consume us in the fire of love that conquers the darkness of the world, a world that has either misunderstood passion or remained passionless. Our experiences here at Manhattan prepare us for this new relationship with the Holy Spirit, this new role we are playing in this world.

But in order to carry out this calling, we, like the disciples in the Upper Room and the Brothers three hundred years ago today, look to Mary, the Spouse of the Holy Spirit, the one who interacted directly with that Love of the Father and the Son. We look to Mary who was the recipient of such Love, which conquers the evil present in our society and in our world. We earnestly seek the Mother of God so that we might carry out the work of Christ. We ask for her help and protection on this day that we, as individuals, as a community, as a College, can be signs of faith in the power of the Holy Spirit.

In the Upper Room that first Pentecost, we read in John's Gospel that Jesus showed the disciples the marks in His hands and His side. Christ's work now has to be carried out by our hands and by our hearts. The Spirit is waiting to assist us in this task. Mary is watching us with the loving eyes of a mother. John Baptist De LaSalle was responding to the Holy Spirit when he called that first General Chapter on the feast of Pentecost in 1694. John Baptist De LaSalle was filled with the Holy Spirit when he said, "Earnestly ask Jesus Christ to make His Spirit come alive in you, since He has chosen you to do His work." *Domine, opus tuum,* which means "Lord, the work is yours," was uttered three hundred years ago, as well as at that first Pentecost. Today the Class of 1994, relying upon the guidance of the Holy Spirit, responds, "That work of Christ is now ours as well."

Addendum II

The Everlasting Character of the Priesthood

There is no doubt that Eugene Hamilton aspired to be "a priest forever." This phrase, which is taken from the description of the Messiah/High Priest in Hebrews 7:17, repeats Psalm 110:4, "a priest forever in the order of Melchizedek," although it directly applies to Christ, has been cherished by priests for centuries as an expression of the permanence of the Sacrament of Holy Orders. Gene put this quotation on his memorial card, which was found in his computer at the time of his death. In doing so he placed himself unequivocally on one side of a present-day theological controversy. His own ordination in the hour of death also affirms most dramatically the tradition of the Church that the Sacrament of Holy Orders makes a permanent change in the person ordained, or to put it more abstractly, an ontological change in the being of the priest. Holy Orders is not simply the assumption of a function as some contemporary theological writers have purported it to be.

A complete discussion of this controversy on the nature of Holy Orders goes quite beyond the purposes of this book — but some acknowledgment of this dispute is necessary for two reasons. The first is the almost shocking way that some theological writers have simply attempted to alter the Church's very important teaching on the priesthood, which touches on several dogmas of the Church. They have done so with little or no acknowledgment, not to say any scruples.

The first important writer to do this was Hans Küng. Father Avery Dulles, S.J., writing in his brief but very illuminating new work, *The Priestly Office*, puts the controversy in clear focus:

> This abrupt departure from a tradition of many
> centuries was bound to provoke some confusion,

if not a crisis. The confusion was compounded by the work of avant-garde theologians, especially in the decade from 1965 to 1975. Not untypical was the book of Hans Küng, *Why Priests?* (published in English in 1972),[1] which called for an abolition of the term "priest" as applied to ministers of the church. According to the New Testament, Küng declared, all believers are priests. Instead of speaking of a ministerial or hierarchical priesthood in the church, he said, we should use functional terms such as "leader" and "presider." The term "hierarchy" should be abandoned. Although bishops and presbyters were the ordinary ministers of the eucharist and of the forgiveness of sins, these sacraments could in cases of urgent necessity be celebrated by charismatically gifted lay persons. Ministerial service, Küng contended, should be open to men and women. The commitment to ministry could be temporary rather than lifelong; there was no justification for the requirement that the ecclesiastical leaders be celibate.

Several of these positions of Küng were rejected by the Congregation for the Doctrine of the Faith (CDF) in the Declaration *Mysterium Ecclesiae* of June 24, 1973 and in a further declaration[2] on Küng's work published on February 15, 1975.[3]

Despite the condemnation of Küng's book, in 1981 Edward Schillebeeckx maintained that in the case of emergency and in the absence of a priest a congregation could designate one of its own members to preside at the Eucharist.[4] Father Dulles continues:

> Schillebeeckx, like Küng, rejected the ontological understanding of the priestly character, which

had been used as a basis for excluding the possibility that the nonordained could celebrate a valid eucharist. Not surprisingly, Schillebeeckx's book on ministry, like Küng's, was disapproved by the Roman Congregation for the Doctrine of the Faith in a letter to the world's bishops on the Ministry of the Eucharist ("*Sacerdotium Ministeriale*") of August 6, 1983.[5] This notification was followed by a letter to Father Schillebeeckx on June 13, 1984,[6] asking him to signify his adherence to the teaching of the previous letter.[7]

Writing precisely on the subject of Schillebeeckx's practical denial of the ordained priesthood, Patrick J. Dunn points out that "one ends up not with theory serving revelation, but with revelation serving a particular theory."[8] Joyce Little, in her review of Schillebeeckx's book *The Church with a Human Face* rightly calls attention to the fact that in the writings of Schillebeeckx on ministry, the "interpreted facts" that he uses "arise out of the theory with which he begins, and necessarily point to the conclusion which his theory already presupposes. This is a fail-safe method for getting to where one wants to go. Unfortunately, it gets there by way of an enormous detour around the facticity of Catholic faith and practice."[9]

The second reason for this addendum is that partially or poorly informed persons pick up ideas like the ones described above and decide that the belief in the permanent character of Holy Orders "went out with Vatican II." This kind of thinking has done much harm to several aspects of Catholic life and in this case has been an important undermining factor in the decrease and loss of priestly vocations. Unfortunately, these ideas are particularly prevalent among those who adopt radical feminist positions and incredibly are imparted to lay people who are in the ministry training programs without giving them the slightest impression that these writings have been officially censured by the Church.

St. Augustine and the Character of Holy Orders

Traditionally, the clear statement that ordination is permanent and irrevocable for the two orders involved in the controversy (bishops and priests, and then by association, deacons) was given by St. Augustine during the Donatist controversy, which raged in North Africa at the beginning of the fifth century. The Donatists were schismatics, originally Catholic Christians, who set up an independent hierarchy because they claimed that other bishops who had surrendered the Scriptures during the persecution of Diocletian had thereby lost not only their Holy Orders, but even their Baptism. The Donatists required that these sacraments had to be received again. St. Augustine staunchly maintained that this was not the traditional teaching or practice of the Church, and that the Donatists had lost sight of the fact that the grace of the sacraments came from Christ independently of the moral worthiness of the minister.[10]

Augustine compared the lasting effect of Holy Orders to that of Baptism and borrowed a term from St. Paul (2 Corinthians 1:22 and Ephesians 1:13; 4:30) who said that the followers of Christ were "sealed" with the Holy Spirit. The Greek term for seal, "*sphragis*," he rendered into Latin as "character," a sacred indestructible sign, not a material but a spiritual reality. He wrote of this character in the three-volume work entitled *Against the Letter of Parmenian*, a successor of Donatus as schismatic bishop of Carthage.[11] Augustine made use of an analogue, the mark or character branded on soldiers of the Roman Legions. He also made use of the fact that if someone was branded without authorization or by trickery, this person was nonetheless a member of the legion and required to serve in it.[12] The character, like that of Baptism or Orders, was irreversible and permanent.

St. Augustine distinguished between the permanence on the one hand and the legitimacy and fruitfulness of Baptism and Holy Orders on the other. He states as the traditional teaching that both sacraments are unrepeatable, and that they can be validly conferred even by those in schism if they have the sacramental authority and use the proper rite. Consequently he admitted the validity of these sacraments when conferred by the Donatists. They did not reciprocate and viciously attacked Augustine, throwing in his face the sinful life that he had confessed to living in his great *Confessions*. For Augustine, the seal or character was distinct from the grace which the sacrament permanently gave unless there was an obstacle on the part of the one who had received it. His sermons on priesthood, collected in the work *We are Your Servants*,[13] make abundantly clear that the personal life and dispositions of the ordained person effected the spiritual fruit they gathered from the sacraments. He teaches that a real bishop is a follower of Christ and lays down his life for the sheep by service and even martyrdom, whereas the other bishops (and priests) who "seek themselves in this high office" are hired hands and have "already received their reward."[14]

Other Fathers of the Church

Other Fathers of the Church — Gregory Nazianzen, Ambrose, John Chrysostom, and Gregory the Great — all wrote about the priesthood and its requirements, discipline, and functions.[15] St. John Chrysostom particularly writes about the office of priest in the New Testament as more august than its Old Testament predecessor. This is because in the Eucharist, the Lord Himself is immolated on the altar and the Holy Spirit descends. He comments that, "Though the office of the priesthood is exercised on earth, it ranks nevertheless, in the order of celestial things — and rightly so. It was neither man nor an angel nor an archangel nor any other created power, but the Paraclete Himself who established this ministry, and who ordained that men abiding in the flesh should imitate the ministry of angels."[16]

St. Thomas Aquinas

The issue of the sacramental character of Holy Orders was not taken up again until the Middle Ages, when the three sacraments (Baptism, Confirmation, and Holy Orders) that leave a character were widely discussed. Although the character was a spiritual reality (and therefore essentially mysterious) it was seen as causing a configuration to Christ and providing specific help or grace to lead a Christian life. In the case of the priesthood it also provided the sacramental powers required for ministry and the performance or conferral of sacraments. St. Thomas Aquinas was clear that Holy Orders brings a spiritual conformity with Christ. Jean Galot, S.J., a Belgian theologian at the Gregorian University, sums up St. Thomas' teaching: "Thomas Aquinas maintains not only that in the priestly character the sacramental character attains to its highest expression but also that character is by its very essence a conformity to the priesthood of Christ even in baptism and confirmation."[17]

Galot takes aim at another minimizing tendency, which attempts again to reduce the priesthood to something less than it is. He writes:

> To make of the priestly character a reduced-scale replica of baptismal character is to espouse a direction alien to the thought of the Church. The priestly character is character in the highest degree, in its most complete realization, the most intense participation in the priesthood of Christ. Thus, the distinctive marks of sacramental character, that is, both the total and the definitive consecration of the person, must be even more pronounced in the priesthood than in baptism and confirmation.[18]

The Protestant Response

The Protestant reformers of course had to attack the whole concept of Holy Orders as a sacrament. Beginning with William Tyndale, they maintained only a priesthood of all Christians. That there was a priesthood of all Christians no one denied, but the reformers denied, in absolute contradiction to the Fathers of the Church beginning with Ignatius of Antioch (A.D. 106), that there was an order of bishops, priests, and deacons. The Catholic Church responded by defining Holy Orders at the Council of Trent. All these decrees can be read with profit, but the one of direct concern to us is as follows:

> But since in the Sacrament of orders, as also in baptism and in confirmation, a sign is imprinted [can. 4], which can neither be effaced nor taken away, justly does the holy Synod condemn the opinion of those who assert that the priests of the New Testament have only a temporary power, and that those at one time rightly ordained can again become laymen, if they do not exercise the ministry of the word of God [can. 1].[19]

Vatican Council II

The whole idea of a true sacramental character, and consequently of the whole sacramental priesthood, has been attacked in varying degrees and ways by some contemporary theological writers as we have seen. The dismissal of the traditional Catholic theology, which belief is substantively shared by the Eastern Orthodox Churches, is a somewhat incredible phenomenon considering the reaffirmation of Holy Orders by Vatican II. In the article on bishops, the decree *Lumen Gentium* (no. 21) says:

> In order to fulfil such exalted functions, the apostles were endowed by Christ with a special

outpouring of the Holy Spirit coming upon them (cf. Acts 1:8; 2:4; Jn. 20:22-23), and, by the imposition of hands (cf. 1 Tim. 4:14; 2 Tim. 1:6-7, they passed on to their auxiliaries the gift of the Spirit, which is transmitted down to our day through episcopal consecration. The holy synod teaches, moreover, that the fullness of the Sacrament of Orders is conferred by episcopal consecration, that fullness, namely, which both in the liturgical tradition of the Church and in the language of the Fathers of the Church is called the high priesthood, the acme of the sacred ministry. Now, episcopal consecration confers, together with the office of sanctifying, the duty also of teaching and ruling, which, however, of their very nature can be exercised only in hierarchical communion with the head and members of the college. In fact, from tradition, which is expressed especially in the liturgical rites and in the customs of both the Eastern and Western Church, it is abundantly clear that by the imposition of hands and through the words of the consecration, the grace of the Holy Spirit is given, and a sacred character is impressed in such wise that bishops, in a resplendent and visible manner, take the place of Christ himself, teacher, shepherd and priest, and act as his representatives (*in eius persona*)."[20]

Although *Lumen Gentium* does not specifically mention the character of ordination for priests, no one would deny that if it is given to bishops it is also given to priests and deacons. Since the entire nature of the priesthood and the role of priests has been under attack by contemporary theological writers, it might be well to review the description of priests given by *Lumen Gentium* (no. 28). It is as follows:

Christ, whom the Father hallowed and sent into the world (Jn. 10:36), has, through his apostles, made their successors, the bishops namely, sharers in his consecration and mission; and these, in their turn, duly entrusted in varying degrees various members of the Church with the office of their ministry. Thus the divinely instituted ecclesiastical ministry is exercised in different degrees by those who even from ancient times have been called bishops, priests and deacons. Whilst not having the supreme degree of the pontifical office, and notwithstanding the fact that they depend on the bishops in the exercise of their own proper power, the priests are for all that associated with them by reason of their sacerdotal dignity; and in virtue of the Sacrament of Orders, after the image of Christ, the supreme and eternal priest (Heb. 5:1-10; 7:24; 9:11-28), they are consecrated in order to preach the Gospel and shepherd the faithful as well as to celebrate divine worship as true priests of the New Testament. On the level of their own ministry sharing in the unique office of Christ, the mediator, (1 Tim. 2:5), they announce to all the word of God. However, it is in the eucharistic cult or in the eucharistic assembly of the faithful (synaxis) that they exercise in a supreme degree their sacred functions; there, acting in the person of Christ and proclaiming his mystery, they unite the votive offerings of the faithful to the sacrifice of Christ their head, and in the sacrifice of the Mass they make present again and apply, until the coming of the Lord (cf. 1 Cor. 11:26), the unique sacrifice of the New Testament, that namely of Christ offering himself once for all a spotless victim to the Father (cf. Heb. 9:11-28).[21]

Addenda

The rest of this number in *Lumen Gentium* examines the duties of priests and then goes on to the diaconate. Since so many seem to think that the traditional Catholic understanding of the priesthood "went out with Vatican II," it might be wise for those interested in the subject to read the entire section in *Lumen Gentium* on Holy Orders.

Priests and Plumbers

Unfortunately Hans Küng and Edward Schillebeeckx are not the only theologians who question the Church's teaching on the priesthood. Along with Küng and Schillebeeckx, one must mention Piet Fransen, who maintained that the Council of Trent did not intend to impose a definition of faith for as long as the Church exists.[22] Piet Schoonenberg maintains that the priestly ministry is a "profession like that of the physician, the engineer, or the plumber."[23] Richard McBrien questions the authenticity of the distinction between clergy and laity. Dunne, who acknowledges that McBrien is trying to encourage the development of ministries in the Church, states that:

> . . . in the process he makes the ordained priesthood appear to be a fourth-century innovation of rather dubious parentage. In doing this he is overlooking the authority so confidently exercised in preceding centuries by the Twelve, by Apostles such as Paul, Timothy and Titus, and by bishops such as Clement of Rome (d. 100) or Ignatius of Antioch (d. 107).[24]

I myself find it amazing that McBrien would adopt this position, which is hardly new. I've been hearing the position that the priesthood was a fourth-century concoction from evangelical and fundamentalist Protestant apologists since I was a teenager preaching for the Catholic Evidence Guild. It's hardly a new idea, but its age certainly does not make it any more valid.

There are several other theological writers who share in a common disdain for the teaching of the Catholic Church on the priesthood. Sadly, these ideas are still passed around uncritically in programs which unconscionably are supported by the alms of the faithful. Father Dulles comments on the prevalence of these ideas twenty years after they have been officially censured by the Church:

> In spite of the disapproval of their positions by the magisterium, theologians such as Küng and Schillebeeckx continued to be very influential with a broad public. Even today, many of the Catholic intelligentsia of Western Europe and the United States either reject the concept of ministerial priesthood or redefine it in ways that make it scarcely distinguishable from the concept of ministry in Protestant Congregationalism.[25]

The Priestly Office

A very fine and succinct summary of the teaching of the Church on the priesthood, as well as of the contemporary theological opinions, is given by Father Avery Dulles in *The Priestly Office*. In language that clarifies so many issues, he summarizes Catholic belief on the being of the priest — a being changed to perform a vocation filled with mystery. Writing specifically on the question of the indelible character of the priesthood, Father Dulles states the following:

> The idea of an indelible character, properly understood, contributes to our understanding of priestly ordination. It implies that this sacrament can never be repeated. Even if a person withdraws from the active ministry, the character remains.

Because of its permanent nature, the character calls for a total and lasting commitment. It grasps the whole being of the person ordained, so that he becomes a man of God, not simply a delegate of the community. The principal agent in ordaining is not the community or even the bishop or bishops; it is Christ the Lord, who confers a share in his own eternal priesthood. As Yves Congar understands it, ordination is "an act of the risen Christ mediated through the already existing office, which is itself in historical continuity with the apostolic community." Because the risen Christ is active in ordination, so is the Holy Spirit. According to Acts 20:28, the presbyter-bishops of Ephesus have been commissioned by the Holy Spirit to feed and guard the flock of Christ.

As I have indicated, there is some debate among contemporary authors about whether the priestly character is ontological or merely functional. In accordance with authoritative teaching on the nature of episcopal consecration, it seems that the character imparted must be in some sense ontological: it is a consecration affecting the new priest in his very being. But the character is also functional in the sense that it is dynamic; it imparts a radical capacity and aptitude to perform certain acts. Metaphysically, I suppose, the character could be described as a spiritual quality, and more technically as a habitus, belonging to the supernatural order.

Ordination imparts a new relationship not only to Christ the head but also to other members of the body of Christ. In particular, it makes one a member of the order of presbyters, who together with the bishops and in subordination to them have responsibility for the communal life of the whole church.[26]

Priest Forever?

Very few theologians have taken up the question of the survival of the priesthood in some way into eternal life. No wonder. St. Augustine reminds us that eye has not seen this everlasting and mysterious reality because it has no color nor has ear heard it because it makes no sound, nor has it entered into our hearts, because our hearts must enter into it.[27] Surely, there will be no pastoral duties for the care of souls for a priest to perform in eternal life, because there is no need. And some may feel that to assume that the priesthood continues on could represent only a silly desire on the part of priests for a first place in heaven. Even the thought that the ontological change denoted by the character of the priesthood may last into eternity could be the origin of a very unpleasant thought, namely, that there is a special hole in hell for the validly ordained, a unique punishment for having abused so great a gift.

But the life and especially the last hours of Eugene Hamilton powerfully bring up the question of priesthood beyond death. Did he become a priest forever, or for only a few hours? As far as we can tell, his only recognizable act of pastoral ministry was to trace a Sign of the Cross, a blessing, into the palm of the hand of a friend. He moved his lips to recite the name of Jesus.

Catholic piety in recent centuries has developed a special devotion around the priesthood. Sometimes this devotion may appear to be largely sentimental, but at other times it may reflect the profound stirrings of the human spirit anointed by grace and confronted by the mysterious gift of Holy Orders. Often we forget that the stirrings of piety are profoundly authentic even though they operate outside the parameters of systematic theology. We should not scoff at that. It is obvious that theology, even pursued by the best of men like St. Thomas Aquinas and St. Bonaventure, was never quite able to cope with a St. Francis, nor has psychology been able to tell us much about the greatness of a St. John Vianney. And who can explain Mary Magdalene, for that matter? A glimpse or two at such non-theological piety might be profitable before we consider two rather solid and startling pieces of theological evidence about what the priesthood may be in eternal life.

The Death of a Priest

The first consideration is that a priest should die a priestly death. If, in fact, a priest is configured to Christ the High Priest and Victim, he should allow this essential component of the priesthood to direct his actions at the hour of death. There is no question that Eugene Hamilton in his partially completed book saw the profound connection between the identity of the priest as victim and the acceptance of a painful physical death. Just as every Christian should strive to die as Christ died, with complete abandonment to God's will and trust in Him, so the priest should exercise his priesthood in the final acts of this earthly life. For all Christians the endurance of the final days of life and the suffering which may accompany them can be a great act of penance and patient expectation.

In a popular meditation book published on the eve of Vatican II, the French priest and spiritual writer Gaston Courtois writes: "By the act of obedience to the all-powerful will of God which it supposes, in union with him who wished to become 'obedient even to death, even to the death of the cross,' we make reparation for all infidelities and for all human rebelliousness."[28]

Courtois suggests to priests that physical sufferings should be accepted in union with the sufferings of Christ. He puts before the priest the powerful icon of the Crucified given by St. Paul in Philippians 2:7: "He emptied himself, taking the form of a slave." Courtois encourages the priest to offer his suffering and death for others:

We can make reparation for all the hate and for the individual and collective selfishness of humanity, by acts of abandonment in union with him who has realized in its fullness the phrase: "Greater love than this hath no one that a man lay down his life for his friends" (John 15:13).[29]

The death of the priest offers a unique opportunity for the witness and service he was called to at ordination when the bishop encouraged him in the words of the rite "to pattern his life on the mystery of the Lord's Cross." Courtois points out that:

It is at the moment of his death that the priest realizes fully his sacerdotal and apostolic ideal, and that he becomes in very truth "the victim of his priesthood," in union with the Victim of Calvary, "for the greater glory of God and for the benefit of all his holy Church."[30]

Gene Hamilton did not offer a First Mass in this life. He did not even offer the actual First Mass of all priests, the one concelebrated with the bishop after the rite of ordination. One might say poetically, but not theologically, that his First Mass was his funeral in the chapel of his beloved St. Joseph's Seminary, where he wore priestly vestments for the first and only time. Here Courtois gives another insight into the mystery of death, the death of a priest. In a moving quotation from Father Perreyve's meditations on Holy Orders, Courtois gives us the following:

Priests should look upon death as one of the last functions of the priesthood. It is their last mass. This mortal body with which you were born at the incarnation was for you, O Jesus, only the material of the sacrifice. This is what this mortal body should be for each of those who share your priesthood. They must make use of it, as you did, to preach the truth, to edify men: but the essential, sacerdotal use they must make of it is to die. They must begin this death in chastity, continue it in mortification, and finish it finally in the true death which is their final oblation and their sacrifice. They should, then, prepare for it as they prepare to celebrate mass, because the death of a priest is a mass, united to your death and consummated in yours for the salvation of mankind.[31]

Although he was not a priest until the last few hours of his life, Eugene Hamilton made a remarkable and profoundly edifying preparation for death as a priest. In ways that are beyond our comprehension or even his, Gene knew that he would be a priest and he prepared for death as a priest. Courtois leaves us with the following profound advice realized in the life of Gene, although he probably never read this book. Father Jules Leo Grimal, in his work, *The Priest and the Sacrifice of Our Lord Jesus Christ*, counsels every priest:

A priest must aim to fulfil the ideal of death, the death of a victim united with Jesus crucified. But let us not wait until the last hour to prepare to make this act of union. . . . Our whole life should be a preparatory exercise for the great act of our death, the act of our supreme sacrifice with Jesus. Perhaps in growing old we shall be frightened by the emptiness, by the poverty, of our sacerdotal life: a life which will seem to us a blank and a failure. The final supreme act can repair much. Let us prepare for this act of reparation. Let us not waste the greatest, the most fruitful moment of our life.[32]

No one reading this book could even think that this life and death was a waste. I wrote this book precisely so that the Christian preparation for death of Eugene Hamilton might be known to as many as possible for their edification and instruction. But even if no line of this book or Gene's own writing was even printed, he had joined Christ in His own sacrificial death, a death by which the Savior had accomplished all things. "I, when I am lifted up from the earth, will draw all men to myself" (John 12:32).

The Eternal Worship

It is an accepted fact of Christianity that the saints in heaven join in the Paschal Mystery of our Lord Jesus Christ in that eternal act of worship by which He, the Head of the human race and of His own Mystical Body, offers to the eternal Trinity the worship of all creation.

There is no doubt that every soul saved by the grace of Christ, whether through the sacraments or in extraordinary ways known to God, participates in that one single act of everlasting worship. It would be absurd to think of different ranks at that time. Ranks are things of human life. Before the Divine Majesty we all stand together as His beloved children. Therefore, why raise the question, does a priest in some special way join in that heavenly mystery because of his participation in the priesthood of Christ through Holy Orders? Does the sacramental configuration to Christ remain in eternal life?

While no one can give a definite answer to that question because it is shrouded in mystery, it will come as a shock to many that two great authors may be cited in favor of the view that in some way a man who is a priest of Christ in this world participates as such in the heavenly mystery. For those who would scoff, the citation of these two immensely powerful authors will give some reason to pause. The two authors are St. Gregory Nazianzen and St. Thomas Aquinas.

First, let's look at the teaching of St. Thomas Aquinas in the *Summa Theologica* (part 3, question 63, article 5). St. Thomas treats directly the question of whether the character of Holy Orders endures beyond death. In this question, he argues that because the character is a sharing in Christ's priesthood, which is eternal, the consecration lasts as long as the thing consecrated. But the soul is indestructible; hence the character must remain forever. In reply to the objection that in heaven there will be no more external worship and consequently the character would be useless (objection 3), Thomas states that the character will remain for the glory or shame of those who used it well or abused it.[33]

In part 3, question 50, article 4, he says directly:

> A man is a priest in his soul, which is marked with the character of orders. By death, then, he does not lose the order of priesthood. Much less then does Christ, who is the source of all priesthood.[34]

St. Thomas cannot be cited as holding that a priest participates in the heavenly liturgy in any specific manner. However, we do have a very interesting quotation from St. Gregory Nazianzen (A.D. 329-390) who preached in A.D. 379 the funeral sermon of St. Basil, the great father of Eastern monasticism and a most popular monk and bishop. In that funeral oration, in order to assuage the grief of the great multitude of people — Christians, Jews, pagans, and strangers — who had come to his funeral, St. Gregory said: Now he is in heaven, and there in our behalf, I am certain, he offers sacrifice and prays for the people.[35]

This is precisely what Eugene Hamilton hoped that he would do in eternal life: He wished to be a priest specifically so that he could join in a priestly way the prayer of the Eternal High Priest offered for the world and for those whom he loved. It is of course a mystery and a question what the eternal life of the saints is like. I must leave it up to you. No dogmatic definition has ever been given and I doubt that one ever will be. Those who wish to scoff at such an idea will no doubt continue to shrug their shoulders, unless perhaps they spend some time in prayer and meditation. Others will have no difficulty at all in accepting that Eugene, in the eternal and endless day of the heavenly Jerusalem, will join the great army of priests in prayer. In fact, we hope he will join all the saints interceding for those who are still involved in the spiritual combat here on earth. Surely all the saints participate in this intercession. We know that St. Thérèse of Lisieux hoped to spend her heaven doing good on earth. St. Gregory and St. Thomas think that priests join in the Paschal Mystery as priests — that is, with a unique conformity to Christ.

I must leave it up to you. Eugene Hamilton was either a priest for less than three hours, or he is a priest forever. Choose your allies and make your choice.

Endnotes

1. Hans Küng, *Why Priests?* (Garden City, N.Y.: Doubleday, 1972).
2. "Vatican Declaration on Hans Küng," *Origins* 4 (March 6, 1975): 577, 579.
3. Father Avery Dulles, S.J., *The Priestly Office: A Theological Reflection* (New York: Paulist Press, 1997), 2-3.
4. Edward Schillebeeckx, *Ministry: Leadership in the Community of Jesus Christ* (New York: Crossroad, 1981), 72-73, 138-39.
5. Congregation for the Doctrine of the Faith, Letter to Bishops, "The Minister of the Eucharist," *Origins* 13 (September 15, 1983): 229-33.
6. Congregation for the Doctrine of the Faith, Letter to Edward Schillebeeckx, "Who can preside at the Eucharist?", *Origins* 14 (January 24, 1985): 523, 525.
7. Dulles, *Priestly Office*, 3.
8. Patrick J. Dunn, *Priesthood: A Re-Examination of the Ro-*

man *Catholic Theology of the Presbyterate* (New York: Alba House, 1990), 43.

9. Quoted in ibid., 44.

10. Jean Galot, S.J., *The Theology of the Priesthood* (San Francisco: Ignatius Press, 1985), 198-201.

11. CSEL 51, 82; PL 43, 72. Cf. *The Retractations*, trans. Sr. M.I. Bogan, Fathers of the Church, vol. 60 (Washington: Catholic University of America Press, 1968), 154-5.

12. Nicholas Haring, S.A.C., "St. Augustine's Use of the Word 'Character,' " Medieval Studies 14 (1952): 81.

13. *We are Your Servants: Augustine on Ministry*, ed. Michael Cardinal Pellegrino (Philadelphia: Augustinian Press, 1986).

14. Ibid., 25.

15. An excellent summary is given by Father Aidan Nichols in *Holy Order: The Apostolic Ministry from the New Testament to the Second Vatican Council* (Dublin: Veritas, 1990), 47-66. This all can be read with great profit.

16. *On the Priesthood*, book 2, chapter 1 and 4; book 4, chapter 5; book 6, chapter 4, cited in ibid., 64.

17. Galot, *Theology of the Priesthood*, 201.

18. Ibid.

19. Council of Trent (1563), in *The Companion to the Catechism of the Catholic Church* (San Francisco: Ignatius Press, 1994), 1580.

20. Text in *Vatican Council II: The Conciliar and Post Conciliar Documents*, ed. Austin Flannery, O.P. (Northport, N.Y.: Costello Publishing Co., 1975), 373-4.

21. Text in ibid., 384-5.

22. Piet Fransen, "Orders and Ordination", in *Sacramentum Mundi*, ed. Karl Rahner et al. (New York: Herder and Herder, 1969), vol. 4, 324-5.

23. Quoted in Galot, *Theology of the Priesthood*, 196.

24. Dunn, *Priesthood*, 23.

25. Dulles, *Priestly Office*, 3-4.

26. Ibid., 12.

27. Letter 130, cited in Father Benedict J. Groeschel, C.F.R., *Augustine: Major Writings, Spiritual Legacy Series* (New York: Crossroad, 1995), 155.

28. Fr. Gaston Courtois, *Before His Face: Meditations for Priests and Religious* (New York: Herder and Herder, 1961), vol. 1, p. 278.

29. Ibid.

30. Ibid.

31. Quoted in ibid., 278-9.

32. Quoted in ibid, 279.

33. *Summa Theologiae: Volume 56: The Sacraments (3a.60-5)*, translator and editor, David Bourke (Cambridge: Blackfriars; New York: McGraw Hill Book Co.; London: Eyre and Spottiswoode, 1975), 91-95.

34. *Summa Theologiae, Volume 54: The Passion of Christ (3a.46-52)*, translator and editor, Richard T. Murphy, O.P. (Cambridge: Blackfriars; New York: McGraw Hill Book Co.; London: Eyre and Spottiswoode, 1965), 129.

35. "On Saint Basil the Great," in *Funeral Orations by Saint Gregory Nazianzen and Saint Ambrose*, translated by Leo P. McCauley, S.J., et al., *Father of the Church*, Volume 22 (New York: Fathers of the Church, Inc., 1953), 97.

Index of Names

Our Sunday Visitor...
Your Source for Discovering the Riches of the Catholic Faith

Our Sunday Visitor has an extensive line of materials for young children, teens, and adults. Our books, Bibles, booklets, CD-ROMs, audios, and videos are available in bookstores worldwide.

To receive a FREE full-line catalog or for more information, call **Our Sunday Visitor** at **1-800-348-2440**. Or write, **Our Sunday Visitor** / 200 Noll Plaza / Huntington, IN 46750.

Please send me: __ A catalog
Please send me materials on:
    __ Apologetics and catechetics   __ Reference works
    __ Prayer books   __ Heritage and the saints
    __ The family   __ The parish

Name_____

Address_____Apt._____

City_____State___Zip_____

Telephone (   )_____

A73BBABP

Please send a friend: __ A catalog
Please send a friend materials on:
    __ Apologetics and catechetics   __ Reference works
    __ Prayer books   __ Heritage and the saints
    __ The family   __ The parish

Name_____

Address_____Apt._____

City_____State___Zip_____

Telephone (   )_____

A73BBABP

Our Sunday Visitor
200 Noll Plaza
Huntington, IN 46750
1-800-348-2440
OSVSALES@AOL.COM

Your Source for Discovering the Riches of the Catholic Faith